I0819317

DESIGN & STYLE MODERN

DRIED FLOWERS

THE ESSENTIAL GUIDE FOR WEDDINGS, EVENTS & THE HOME

Sarah Ogden

DESIGN & STYLE MODERN DRIED FLOWERS

THE ESSENTIAL GUIDE FOR WEDDINGS, EVENTS & THE HOME

THE CROWOOD PRESS

Contents

Introduction

Do you wish you could enjoy your flowers all year without having to worry about replacing their murky water or watching them die? I'm here to tell you that not only can you keep your flowers, but they can also look beautiful, vivid and colourful for years. Welcome to the wonderful new world of dried flowers.

I've been working with dried and preserved flowers for over five years now. My original plan had been to open my own fresh floristry wedding design studio, and I even trained with fresh florals before I came across what I describe as modern dried flowers. I was instantly hooked. I'm completely biased as I spend my days surrounded by dried flowers, but I honestly cannot understand why anyone would want fresh florals now.

Back in the day, dried flowers were exactly that – dried-up flowers. They were left to dry, and they turned brittle, brown and lifeless. While they had a moment of trending in the 1970s, they never really offered anything different or special. Since then, there have been many advancements in the dried flower world. Twenty-first century dried flowers are no longer dull; there are now hundreds of varieties of dried, painted and dyed flowers – and most recently there has been a boom in the preserved floral arena. In this book, I will introduce you to a world of dried and preserved flowers in a stunning array of colours, from beautiful pale tones all the way through the colour wheel to bright and bold shades.

For me, preserved florals are the big game changer. Some flowers have small, delicate stems, while other flower heads are larger and more impactful, but all have huge amounts of texture. Now you can have big blousy blooms that are soft to the touch, have amazing colour and look and feel like fresh flowers, but that don't wither and die. I'm thrilled to be able to share all the knowledge and experience I have gathered from working with this wonderful medium, making the joy of flowers stay with you for longer. I will give you all the tools you need to set your own style and create your floral dreams with confidence for your home, wedding or special event.

About This Book

This book is broken down into three main parts. In the first part, Design It, I will help you explore all you need to know to get started, from the tools you will require all the way through to the different types of flowers and foliage you can choose from, as well as teaching you where to find your inspiration and how to choose your own floral style. I will then teach you some foundational techniques that will help you with your creations, including the spiral technique (*see* page 30), how to tape flowers (*see* page 32) and how to wire and reflex preserved flower heads (*see* pages 34 and 36).

The second part, Create It, contains all the tutorials you will need to construct your designs. We look first at wedding flowers, with step-by-step projects for all the bridal party, including styles for the wedding bouquet (*see* page 42), bridesmaid bouquets (*see* page 61), buttonholes (*see* page 73), and corsages and accessories (*see* page 80). We can then conquer displays for your rooms and events, with a lovely trio of bud vases (see page 100) and gorgeous table and floor-standing arrangements (*see* page 106). At the end of this part, we will go deeper into your newfound knowledge and learn a few more complicated arrangements and installations with serious wow factor, including a flower cloud (see page 124) and decorated arch (*see* page 128).

In the final part, Style It, my aim is to give you all the tools you need to style your arrangements simply and to perfection. We will look at the trimmings – vases, bows and ribbons – that will give your creations the perfect professional finishing touch, as well as the best ways to cut, wrap and hold your bouquets for maximum appeal.

At the end of sections two and three you will find Q&As with industry experts, to give you all the insider tips and knowledge you need to help you on your way.

Finding a lovely space to work in is important as you work creatively. Use a space with a natural light source, if possible. You need to be able to see the flowers to check their colours work together and to see what you have at your disposal to work with.

Why Choose Dried and Preserved Flowers?

The one thing my couples tell me time after time is that they want to be able to keep their wedding flowers – and why shouldn't they? Planning an event is an expensive thing to do, and weddings now cost more than ever. The idea that you would spend so much money on fresh flowers that will die within days of your event is not something that can be easily squared away with today's consumers. This book will give you all the knowledge you need to create your own dried or preserved wedding or event flowers, saving you a lot of money as well as inspiring you to be as creative as possible.

Dried and preserved flowers are not what they used to be; there has been an explosion of newness into the market and they now come in many different forms. Yes, you can have dried pampas and fluffy grasses such as wheat, feather grass and bunny tails, but now you can also have colourful wildflowers, daisies, roses, big-headed hydrangeas and bold blooms such as protea and achillea. Previously, you would have had lots of limitations with the colour and varieties available to you, meaning your designs would have needed to follow what was narrowly available. Now, colour limitations are no longer an issue; dried flowers come in a rainbow of shades and tones and there are new varieties becoming available all the time (*see* page 26 for a list of the various dried flowers I like to use in my designs).

Dried flowers are available either dried in their natural state (some varieties come in beautiful natural colours that dry so well the colour is retained) or dried and then dyed or painted into an array of lovely colours. I like to use a variety of types in my designs, depending on the colour depth I am looking to achieve. Some stems are light and delicate and others are thick and strong. Wildflower-style naturally foraged designs look better with lots of delicate stems, while bold floral-heavy designs suit stronger, larger-headed flowers.

Sustainability and Environmental Advantages

As we move towards a more sustainable future, we are all looking for ways to be more thoughtful as we consume. Flowers are not very eco-friendly if they are produced in any other way than grown in your back garden. Even packets of seeds can be produced abroad and flown into the country. Bringing mountains of fresh flowers into the country from many thousands of miles away, when they last only a few days, is certainly not ideal.

You can enjoy dried flowers for years after your event, meaning there is no need to buy fresh flowers and replace them week-in, week-out. Bridesmaid bouquets can be given as gifts, buttonholes turned into keepsakes and table centrepieces used to decorate your home, or reused for your next event. With dried and preserved flowers the consumption level is drastically reduced – and that can only be a good thing.

What Is the Difference Between Dried and Preserved Flowers?

Dried flowers are exactly what they say they are: flowers that are dried. They are more brittle and delicate and feel quite hard to the touch.

Preserved flowers are a whole new world of floristry as they also last for years because they are treated with glycerine, which preserves the flowers and stops them from drying out. Preserved flowers are soft to the touch and retain their beautiful natural colours or can be dyed. It is possible to preserve your own flowers to achieve this look (*see* page 15).

My Favourite Flowers

My absolute favourite flower is the mighty hydrangea – what beautiful large, fluffy blooms they have! Preserved versions of this flower come in a stunning array of colours too. My favourite colour has to be pale pink but I do have a soft spot for this flower in dark, inky tones such as burgundy and deep teal.

Funnily enough, my favoured dried flowers are completely opposite to my preserved favourites. When dried, I like smaller, delicate-headed flowers such as the lovely rhodanthe with its teeny daisy-like flower heads on the spindliest of stems. This can be added in bunches and adds a lovely movement – I'm always striving to get as much movement into my designs as possible, so I love dried flowers like these.

Other flowers that I adore and which add lots of drama and movement to my designs are oats and ferns. You can read more about these stems, and many more, in Part One (*see* page 26).

Dried flower bouquets can be stored for many months before you need to use them. Once you have created your design, storing them upright allows you to ensure that they don't get flattened. Bouquets can also stand upright on their own, sitting on the stems if you cut them straight at the bottom.

PART ONE: DESIGN IT

Getting Started

Before you get started with your dream florals, not only do you need to mentally prepare yourself for a lot of work, you will also need to get organised with the right tools. This part of the book will help to guide you through the preparation stage with ease.

Before we get to the practical side of things, I suggest you have a moment or two to sit down and plan everything out. Try to involve friends and family in this process. You could make it part of the event planning – perhaps you have a floral arranging class with your friends in lieu of a more traditional hen (bachelorette) party, or maybe you want to arrange a dinner where everyone has a go at making a little bud vase arrangement.

You can never practise too much; the more you practise in advance, the easier the whole process will be. Trust your ideas, have fun and know that not everything has to be perfect – your guests will never know if something isn't quite as you'd planned.

Tool Kit

Before you get started, you will need to arm yourself with a few important tools. You will find other things that help you and that you love too, but these are the basics that I use over and over and rely upon most days when I'm creating my flowers.

1. **Secateurs** – Invest in a decent pair of secateurs, or as I call them, 'clippers'. I can't stress enough how important this one tool will be for you. Some of the thicker stems can be very tough to cut through, and this task is made all the more difficult if your clippers aren't sharp enough.
2. **Wire cutters** – I use wire cutters every time I'm using floral bind wire, which is for every bouquet at the minimum. The ones I use came free when I bought my rolls of chicken wire, so they are not top of the range by any means. You just need something that can snip through those wires (you don't want to blunt your clippers by using them).
3. **Floral bind wire** –This very strong paper-coated wire can be easily bent with your fingers. Essential for wrapping bouquets, I also use it to hang floral clouds.
4. **Florist coated wire** – Long lengths of coated wire that come in different shades of green and white. I use this for making flower crowns.
5. **Fishing wire** – This is great for hanging clouds as it almost disappears from a distance. It is also very strong and will hold a heavy flower cloud.
6. **Galvanised stub wire** – I use 26 gauge for wiring my preserved flower heads (*see* page 34). It comes in different weights, but get the strongest or thickest you can to avoid it bending.
7. **Chicken wire** –I use the smallest mesh size possible, but you can fold it over itself to make smaller holes if you need to.
8. **Scissors** – I have a pair for cutting papers and a separate little sharp pair for cutting ribbons. Don't blunt your sharp ones by cutting paper!
9. **Glue** – For securing flowers to ribbons and sticking ribbon ends down. I use UHU as it is easy to use and effective.
10. **Floral tape** – Available in white and green, this is great for taping your preserved flower heads and loose stems into bunches to create larger blooms. I use green for darker colours and white for lighter ones.
11. **Stapler** – I use this when wrapping my flower bunches in paper and securing them.
12. **Floral spray paints** – Floral sprays are perfect for adding a touch of the colour you want or a golden or

There is no need to spend a fortune on your tools. Most items can be purchased relatively cheaply from local hardware shops or online. You will use some items much more than others. The only item that is worth spending a little more on is your secateurs – they must be very sharp to cut through some of the dried stems.

Drying your own flowers is really easy to do. Some varieties dry much easier than others, so have a go with different varieties and see what works best. At the very least they will look beautiful hanging in your space.

glitter finish to a palm leaf or some stems of wheat. You can also use them to create an ombre effect where the colour of the ends of the stems fades down to nothing, giving just a hint of colour on the edges.

13. **Pens** – I'm old school and I like to write everything down!
14. **Sweeping brush** – For cleaning up – dried flowers make *a lot* of mess!
15. **Gloves** – Great for protecting your hands when working with wires (chicken wire can be especially sharp once cut). Wear gloves when working with floral foam, as the little loose fibres can be unpleasant.

Floral Foam

Floral foam has become a hot topic in recent years for very good reason. Your typical floral foam, also known as Oasis®– the green blocks of foam that can be used dry or holds water for fresh flowers – has come under scrutiny of late. It's now known to be extremely damaging for the environment, with its microplastics disappearing into the water system and polluting our natural resources.

I do not use this kind of floral foam in my designs, but have sourced an environmentally friendly alternative. There are a few companies in the market that produce an eco-alternative foam, which is made from natural fibres that are designed to break down naturally and can be composted.

Drying and Preserving Flowers

Drying your own flowers is really easy and there are a number of floral varieties that dry very well. You can use flowers that you have grown in your own garden (I once happily discovered a patch of honesty growing wild in my garden) or flowers that you have been gifted and are on their way out, or you can purchase fresh flowers with a plan to dry them yourself. I dry a few different varieties that I order in, but if I had more time I would dry additional types.

Drying Flowers

Flowers that work really well for drying yourself are: gypsophila, ferns, helichrysum, statice, oats, wheat and honesty. To dry flowers yourself:

1. First separate the stems as best as you can so that they are not intertwined too much – if you try to separate each stem once they are dry, they will more than likely break.
2. Gather the stems into bunches and wrap with a little floral bind wire or ribbon lengths around the end of the stems.
3. Hang them upside down in a dry place, out of direct sunshine. The stems will usually dry in a couple of weeks.

Preserving Flowers

It's also possible to preserve your own flowers. This method can be a little hit or miss and definitely works better for smaller-headed flowers, but give it a go – you never know your luck!

1. Start by filling a few large vases with one part 100 per cent natural glycerine and two-parts hot boiling water. Stir the liquid until the glycerine is dissolved.
2. Prepare your stems. With fresh flowers, it's a good idea to remove all the leaves that go down the stems and focus on the blooms only, so the leaves don't rot in the water and make a gunky mess.
3. Cut the ends of the stems cleanly at a 45-degree angle. This is so there is a wider surface at the bottom for the flowers to 'drink up' your glycerine solution.
4. Pop your flowers into the vases and leave them there for a week. If they 'drink up' all the solution, make some more and add that to the vase. After they have been in the vase for a week, carefully remove them, tie them at the end with a ribbon or floral wire and hang them upside down for a couple of weeks.

Storing Dried Flowers

Your floral creations can last for years if you care for them properly (this includes the stems before you arrange with them, and the arrangements afterwards). First and foremost, dried flowers must be kept dry. Do not place them in a room that has a lot of moisture in the air, such as a bathroom or kitchen. Keep your flowers away from bright and direct sunlight, which can bleach the colour from the stems.

Dried flowers tend to arrive from the floral merchants without plastic wrap, in brown boxes, while fresh flowers often arrive wrapped in plastic, which is almost impossible to recycle or reuse. This is another reason why I prefer to work with dried flowers; I am able to either reuse or recycle all the brown boxes so the waste is very minimal. I keep my stems in these boxes until I am ready to use them, or in large buckets that are out of sunlight if I need to see what stock I have on hand. After your event, you can either break down the flowers and store all the stems for use in a future arrangement, or keep your arrangements in boxes out of sunlight until you have decided what you are going to do with them.

Storing your dried flowers correctly is important for ensuring that they retain their colour and appearance. Dried flowers will last for years if stored properly, so make sure they are out of sunlight and damp conditions.

A beautiful space to work in can be very inspiring. Get all your flowers out and look at them together before you start working with them. Put a few inspirational pictures up on the wall and make your space reflect the look you want to achieve.

Being Inspired

Designing flowers is a creative process. There is a lot to think about before you begin, so set yourself up with all the background knowledge you need to get creative. I find the whole process to be quite methodical in its nature – I think of it as building blocks that I build onto. I start with an idea for a project then I research it and collate ideas that blossom as the concept forms. All of this happens before I even pick up a single stem. Over the next few pages I am going to give you a breakdown of these building blocks so you can build your own floral dream.

Looking for Inspiration

Back in 2012, when I started my floral journey with the somewhat daunting task of making my own wedding flowers without any training or even research, I created a whole concept from one flower. I just knew I wanted yellow billy balls in my design. This is really funny to think about now because this is a flower that dries incredibly well but that I don't use at all; I'm not sure why but I've moved on. Trends come and go and your ideas change over time, and that is all part of the wonderful creative process.

It sounds corny to say this, but inspiration really is all around us. You can look to popular culture or nature, but the most useful inspiration these days can be quite literal – look at what other people are doing and see if you like it. I'm not asking you to copy other people's work, I'm merely suggesting that you look at what is out there and use that as a base for your ideas. You can, and should, adapt everything you see; meld multiple ideas and themes together or take one little aspect from something you've seen and build out from it.

Pinterest is an invaluable source of ideas. Its clever algorithm means that it will continue to show you ideas around a theme. So, start pinning and making little folders of all the things you love. Even if it feels as though you love everything and your ideas are too far and wide to hone into one theme, over time you will start to see the things you tend to navigate towards more often.

Instagram is also a wonderful place to see what other creatives are doing. Most creatives share their work to inspire others; again, the algorithm will see what you love and show you more of this. Instagram is also amazing at allowing you to see a little behind the scenes of what it takes to create beautiful work; it might give you an idea that will start your theme. Being online also helps you avoid the seasonal blues – even in the darkest depths of winter, you can see summery colours from Australia – so, you can still plan a summer event in January.

Wedding and event stylists are another amazing resource for you to spend some time researching. They provide lots of free inspiration and concepts for you, from the simple and achievable to fabulous celebrity events with sky-high budgets.

For my creative process, I like to start with colour first. Gather images from all of the colour combinations you like – this might be a fashion or beauty magazine spread that shows an amazing combination of colours, or a more literal example of a wedding that jumped out to you. Once you have an idea of the colours you want to use, you can search dried and preserved floral supplier websites for what is available in the colours you like. I feel my most inspired when I'm looking at the actual flowers, so spend a little time seeing what is available and even pop a few items in your cart. (Beware, if you are using an online floral merchant's website, direct from the market, they update their stock in-the-minute, and once an item is in your cart you are agreeing to purchase it. So, make your selections before you add to cart.)

Think About Shape, Colour and Texture

There are three main principles to consider when creating your designs: shape, colour and texture. As one affects the other, all of these principles feed into each other. You should consider the sizes and scales of your florals, which flowers you are using and what you want to focus on. Is there a specific flower that you love and you'd like to build your design around? Do you have favourite colours to focus on? Are you after a look or a feeling?

The size of your flower arrangements plays into your budget. Do you want to go all out with huge floral displays or are you keen to keep things simpler? There are ways to cheat things a bit here – larger displays could be made with more cost-effective flowers, saving your expensive focal flowers for your bouquet or one or two choice pieces.

Do you want your flowers to be fluffy and romantic (choose ferns and pampas grasses), bold and contemporary (focus on bold colour stories and big-headed blooms such as roses and hydrangea) or soft and drapey (use flowers and foliage with lots of natural movement, such as eucalyptus nicholii and dried wheat)? Think also about the shape; fluffy pampas looks great in asymmetrical designs, while classic designs featuring roses and foliage work well when there is a better symmetry.

Deciding Your Floral Style

All of my designs have a natural and relaxed feel as this is my preferred style, but there is still a huge variance between my different styles, depending on the shape and the flowers used. My designs fall into four main categories:

1. ***Classic romantic*** – A versatile style that can be adjusted to be more or less relaxed in its construction; essentially this is a classic, contemporary design that is even in its design and floral placement. Flowers and foliage are used together to create this style, which can range from using four or five floral components and having a simple design to using a much wider variety of stems for a more uneven appearance. The shape is slightly rounded and even. You can make this as tightly packed as you want, but I make it slightly relaxed and open.
2. ***Boho luxe*** – Designs feature pampas and fluffy grasses as the main component, which can be combined with roses or kept simple with dried grasses. You can make this design in a rounded shape or go for more dramatic, asymmetrical designs.
3. ***Relaxed wildflower*** – This design is made using all dried flowers, and it can be colourful or more natural and rustic in its colour palette. The stems are smaller-headed flowers that have a wild, naturally foraged look. I design with an even construction, adding flowers through the design so that they blend together perfectly. My style favours the more colourful look as I love to create interesting and impactful palettes, but it works well in neutrals too.
4. ***Flower heavy*** – A modern design that is made with mostly large-headed preserved flowers such as roses and hydrangea. I do sometimes add little touches of other dried flowers or pampas to this design, but the main focus of the shape is the big-headed blooms. This also works really well in bold or clashing colours, as well as adding even more drama through colour blocking.

Think about your own style and how much you would like it to affect your floral style. Are you a gregarious person who likes to be the centre of attention? If so, you may want a bold floral style such as flower heavy. Or are you a more relaxed, bohemian person who would look much more at home with a boho-luxe-style bouquet?

Think About Your Venue, Budget and Timings

Along with your own personal style, it is important to think about where your flowers will be. Is your venue rustic with lots of character? Would wildflower-inspired creations work well in a barn setting? Or is your venue classically stylish, so a classic and romantic design would work better? As you plan your room or event flowers, think about which items would work best in the space – does your venue have a blank wall that would look good with a hanging cloud or lots of long tables that you need to dress?

Consider your budget and how many items you can afford to make. If your venue is really large and there are a lot of tables, perhaps something more affordable like

A soft, romantic bridal bouquet with lots of roses and pampas grass for a fluffy, feminine look. This bouquet is rounded in its shape but I played with the heights of the pampas to give it a more relaxed feel.

Asymmetrical boho-style bouquets are beautiful in natural tones but also work well in palettes with lots of different colours. This is a pastel-toned bouquet with pink pampas grass, trailing ferns and large hydrangea heads.

Wildflower bouquets work well in a rainbow colour story. It can be nice to use lots of different varieties to make up a wildflower combination that gives the arrangement the appearance of naturally foraged flowers collected from hedgerows.

Flower-heavy bouquet designs are dramatic and eye-catching, especially if you choose bright and bold clashing colours. Use multiple tones of the same colour for a dynamic look, ranging from pale pink to hot pink and deep red to light crimson.

Selecting the right stems is a wonderful part of the creative process and can really kickstart your concepts. Spend time looking at flowers, understand the different tones that they are available in and mix and match varieties. Spend time researching what is available to you and buy flowers in advance.

bud vases would work well. Or if your event is an intimate dinner for ten to twenty people and you want your tables to have more impact, you could opt for table centrepieces. If you need to fill a lot of space, think about the floral style too. Large preserved blooms are more expensive to buy than dried flower stems but maybe you won't need as many to create impact. Consider the total event budget that you want to apply to your flowers; perhaps you want to focus more on your flowers and less on your signage or forgo a cake or videographer.

Finally, when should you start your project? This depends greatly on how many pieces you plan to make and how difficult they are to master (a flower cloud or archway may be more challenging and take a few attempts to get right). The most important thing to remember is to allow more than enough time; nobody wants to be stressing or rushing at the last minute when they have other things to think about. Don't forget, dried and preserved flowers can be made well in advance and kept until you are ready.

Choosing Your Colour Story

My favourite part of the concept creation is coming up with a beautiful colour story. Colour palettes are so important; even a neutral colour combination has perfect shades that work best together. There is a wealth of information available on the internet for using complementary colour palettes and colour wheels, but I find it much better to source an image that you like and work from that. Pinterest has loads of images available that show lovely colour stories you can use as a starting point.

To help you narrow down your colour intention, ask yourself these important questions:

- Do you want colour or neutral?
- Do you want to focus on one colour or on a selection of colours?
- Do you want to include green foliage throughout or focus on your flowers?
- Do you want to keep things classic (white, ivory, pink) or go for something more dramatic?
- Do you have a favourite colour you want to focus your ideas around?

Even though you don't need to worry about seasonally available flowers when you work with dried flowers, since different colours and styles are available all year or you can store them until needed, it can still be helpful to reference the season of your event. For example, summer weddings are lovely when very colourful, while autumnal weddings work well with muted rust and natural tones.

Below is a list of my favourite colour stories to get you thinking or inspire you:

- **Palest of pale** – White, cream and ivory (optionally, add in touches of blush pink, sage green or foliage).
- **Pastel tones** – Pale pink, lilac, peach, baby blue and duck-egg blue (optionally, add in touches of pale yellow).
- **Rainbow** – All the shades of the rainbow. I like to focus on the warmer, more natural tones such as pink, purple and orange and add touches of navy blue for a nice contrast.
- **Warm tones** – Pick a few tones from the warm family – reds, pinks, oranges and rusts. This is perfect for an autumnal event, and you could add in some warm browns and foliage too. Remember to use multiple tones of the same colour for more depth.
- **Cool tones** – Pastel shades of blue, navy, greens and yellows (add ivory and foliage to soften the look here too).
- **Deep, dark gothic** – Use blacks, greys and dark shades of brown, red or burgundy.

Use the above concepts as a base and add in one unexpected pop of colour – maybe a yellow ochre, neon pink or deep burgundy. Adding that pop of colour makes your palette really sing.

Seasonal Inspiration

While there are fewer limitations for seasonality when working with dried flowers, it's still important to consider the season when you are designing your floral concept. I often get couples asking if it will be a problem to use certain flowers for their wedding because of the season. This isn't a problem at all for dried flowers! While there are some seasonal availability issues – for example, it can be hard to get hold of eucalyptus in the back end of the year – this isn't a problem as you can buy your stems when they are available and store them until you need them.

If you are having a hard time coming up with your colour story, you could revert to the seasonal norms to give you an idea. It's also nice to have flowers that work for the season, so if it is autumn and the leaves outside are changing into all those beautiful colours, it is nice if your flowers reflect that. Or, if it is sunny in high summer, a bright and colourful palette always works wonderfully. I'm not one to work too closely with the norms as I like unexpected colours, so feel free to use the following seasonal colour palettes purely as inspiration for any time of the year, for any event.

Spring Colour Palette

I wanted to create an unusual colour palette that was light, airy and pretty. This kind of palette would work beautifully for a spring wedding as it is fresh, light and softly colourful.

The colours in this palette range from pale peach to pink, with highlights of light yellow and two tones of blue – a duck-egg hydrangea and a brighter blue wheat. I like to use multiple tones of one colour, so adding the brighter blue gives a lively contrast and depth to the palette; the same applies to the pale peach offset with the coral. I also used a blue-toned eucalyptus that fit beautifully with the blues in the rest of the palette.

STEMS USED

- Peach ruscus
- Peach PeeGee hydrangea
- Coral phalaris
- Pale pink hydrangea
- Yellow statice
- Duck-egg blue hydrangea
- Pale blue wheat
- Blue-green eucalyptus cinerea
- White gypsophila

A spring colour palette tends to be light and bright to reflect the season. Using soft pastel tones back to ivory ensures a light and airy colour story. Introducing lots of gypsophila breaks up the design and adds a lovely open look to the flower arrangement.

Summer Colour Palette

My favourite colour stories for summer are bright and colourful. Summer events just work so well with vivid colours, while the sun is shining and we have lovely long evenings. Bright colours also complement everyone's more upbeat spirit during the summer.

I tend to gravitate towards warm colour palettes with pinks and reds, so this palette is made up of a collection of my favourite shades, ranging from pale pinks and lilacs all the way through to deep burgundy and pops of bright orange. I like to use multiple tones of the same colour; here we have three pink tones that range from a dusky mid-pink to hot-pink bunny tails, two tones of lilac and pale purple, and two tones of orange: a muted rust palm and hot-pink gypsophila.

STEMS USED

- Lilac phalaris
- Pale purple statice
- Pink dyed palm cups
- Pink preserved gypsophila
- Hot-pink bunny tails
- Bright orange dried gypsophila
- Muted orange palm leaves
- Burgundy ruscus

Summer colour palettes are the perfect time to be bold, bright and vivid. I love to use bright hot tones of pink and orange in summer, mirroring the weather and the optimism of the time of year. We spend the most time outdoors in summer and a bright colour story reflects this.

Autumn Colour Palette

The autumn season brings about a lot of change in the outdoors – leaves changing colour and falling from trees, the weather turning cool, fires being lit and people hunkering down indoors. It can be lovely to reflect this seasonal change in your colour palette for weddings and events. At this time of the year I get asked a lot for foliage-heavy designs with autumnal shades of flowers, and there are a few of these palettes within this book for you to reference.

For this specific colour palette I wanted to offer you an idea of something a little lighter and less serious. This colour story is how I would approach the autumn season, adding in a little of my signature pink and warm colour story. This palette begins with the lightest pink for the large palm leaves and goes right through to a deep terracotta hydrangea. I introduce peaches, brighter oranges and rusts for a whole range of the orange colour family, as well as an amazing gypsophila that is both hot pink and bright orange, which I dried myself.

STEMS USED

- Pale pink large palm leaves
- Pink preserved hydrangea
- Pink and orange dried gypsophila
- Peach bunny tails
- Orange achillea
- Bright orange oats
- Rust preserved hydrangea
- Rust broom bloom

As well as a time for hunkering down and getting cosy, autumn is fast becoming one of the busiest times of the year to get married. Couples are loving the fact that they can blend the historically autumnal season with the amazing weather of the summer, and have a colour story reflecting that.

Winter Colour Palette

For winter colour stories, I like to use a lot of ivory and white and I mix in some deeper and darker tones for a lovely contrast. I also like to do all-white colour palettes – these would be made with white, ivory and natural tones so the palette still has a lot of different shades, textures and interest within it.

This winter colour story has a base of light ivory with some white highlights. I layer on soft natural-toned pampas, which adds some texture too. Onto this, I layer my colours that add depth – these are all warmer in their tone and range from the palest pink to natural burgundy, deep saturated burgundy and eucalyptus leaves in a deep reddish brown. This high-contrast colour palette still has a lot of softer tones to make sure it remains really pretty.

STEMS USED

- Ivory broom bloom
- White oats
- White thistle
- Natural pampas grass
- Pale pink billy balls
- Pale pink bunny tails
- Natural dried nigella
- Burgundy preserved hydrangea
- Red eucalyptus populus

Winter is the perfect time to inject some icy whites into your colour palette – it is cold outside so it's nice to mirror that frostiness with some cool whites. I add touches of colour among them to soften the look and add interest. Deep foliage colours are also lovely at this time of the year.

Selecting Flowers and Foliage

Let's talk about all the flower varieties that are available to you. I love to build out my concepts once I select my stems. I can spend hours searching my suppliers' websites (*see* page 157) for different varieties and unusual colours. Most suppliers stock the basic dried stems but they occasionally get new or interesting varieties in stock. When they do, I snap them up and keep hold of them for future designs; they may never come back in stock otherwise.

Dried Flowers and Grasses

Below is a selection of my favourite stems to use. These are available in many different colours and shades. There are many more varieties of dried flowers available, but here are a selection of my favourite and most useful ones:

- **Achillea** – Lovely long, strong stems (the offcut stems are useful for wiring rose heads, so save these for later) with large heads of varying sizes. Makes a really great focal flower as it comes painted in lots of different colours.
- **Broom bloom** – An extremely useful flower that I use as a base for most of my bouquet designs. This flower comes in bunches that look like bushes; it's very sturdy and is a great filler. Comes in a huge variety of painted and dyed colours as well as bleached white and natural (brown).
- **Bunny tails (lagurus ovatus)** – Who doesn't love a bunny tail? This stem is the sweetest – long fine stems with a little puff of fluff on the end. Available in a huge array of fun colours as well as natural beige stems.
- **Delphinium** – A long-stemmed flower that has little flowers all down the length of its stem. This makes it rather an unusual stem so it definitely adds something different to your arrangements. It comes in natural blue, white or pink stems.
- **Feather grass** – Exactly what it sounds like, this stemmed grass can add a lovely little extra fluff to your arrangements. Available in lots of dyed colours, it's light, airy and smoother in its texture than pampas grass.
- **Gypsophila** – Another flower that most people adore. Its little sprays of flowers are a great filler because they add lots of texture, available in natural white as well as different dyed and sprayed varieties. I dry my own (*see* page 15 for how to do this yourself).
- **Helichrysum (strawflower)** – A lovely flower that comes in lots of natural shades, from white to natural shades of pink, bright reds to oranges. This is a variety of the chrysanthemum so it has nice big flowers, but it is delicate so the stems can break easily. Save any damaged heads for other crafting projects.
- **Lavender** – We all know and love lavender, don't we? It dries beautifully and still smells so lovely and fragrant. It is super delicate, though, and you will inevitably lose quite a few flowers from each stem as you work with it.
- **Lepidium** – Long grassy dried stems with little beaded leaves all the way down. Adds a lovely natural green colour to your arrangements.
- **Oats (avena)** – Long, strong stems available in a huge array of colours. This stem adds great movement and texture to your arrangements and is almost feathery in its shape.
- **Palm cup** – A great focal flower with large dried heads. Available in quite a few painted colours as well as natural brown and bleached ivory.
- **Palm leaves (palm spears)** – Large palm leaves that are cut into different shapes, varying from extra-large, wide, semicircular shapes to smaller triangular shapes. Available in many painted, dyed colours as well as natural and bleached ivory.
- **Pampas grass** – Big plumes of fluffiness with very long, strong stems. These can be split into smaller pieces – just break off chunks and tape them onto discarded stems. Pampas is naturally a light beige colour that gets paler and fluffier as it dries out. It also comes dyed in many different shades. I use a lot of natural pampas and the occasional pink or orange stem.
- **Phalaris (canary grass)** – Lovely pops of colour! It has little balls of dried grass heads on the end of long stems and comes in bunches of hundreds of stems. A useful stem that adds nice movement to your arrangements and is available in lots of different dyed and painted colours.
- **Protea repens** – This large dried flower originates from South Africa but has a slightly tropical look to it. There are a few different varieties of protea, but I like the repens version best as it is slightly open and looks

more attractive. Other varieties have a slightly alien look to them, so I avoid them.

- **Rhodanthe** – Bunches of beautiful! These little flowers on spindly fine stems look a lot like daisies and come in two natural colours: white and pink, both with yellow centres.
- **Statice** – A gorgeous stem that is easy to dry yourself and adds great colour to your arrangements. It's available in quite a few natural colours: white, yellow and shades of pink and purple. It can be quite spiky in parts, so be careful when handling this flower.
- **Thistle (teasel)** – Large thistle heads are available in a range of natural, bleached or dyed stems. It is very spiky on the stems, so be extra careful when handling these. I like to scrape off all the spikes on the stems before I begin arranging with this flower.
- **Wheat (triticum)** – A sturdy stem available in a rainbow of colours that adds structure to your designs.

Preserved Flowers

There are many more varieties of preserved flowers now available, including carnations, dahlia and sunflowers. Here is a list of the flowers that I have found to work best and I use the most in my designs.

- **Garden roses** – A slightly different version of the classic rose, the garden rose is more closed up with frillier petals and looks like a peony before it opens up. Adds variance to your preserved florals.
- **Gardinia** – A flatter flower with slightly curled petals. It looks really pretty as an alternative to roses and has a good surface area.
- **Gypsophila** – Absolutely gorgeous when it is preserved as it retains almost all of its natural charm. You can preserve it yourself (*see* page 15). It also comes ready-preserved in a stunning array of bright colours such as neon pink, bright teal, yellows and pinks. Gypsophila adds lots of texture to your arrangements and can be used at the edges of bouquets for extra movement.
- **Hydrangea** – An absolute favourite flower of mine. Big blousy blooms with lovely little petals that come in a huge colour range. These are available in a variety of sizes but the blooms are large and can be split into a few smaller heads to make them easier to use. You can also use little pieces that come off (or are removed) for buttonholes, corsages, flower crowns and other smaller items.
- **Moss** – A useful base for your designs. Comes in a large variety of dyed colours as well as bleached white.
- **Mum Kotonegiku** – Small flowers with pink centres that look a little like a chrysanthemum. The stems are really fine, adding a different, delicate touch to your designs.
- **Roses** – A preserved floral staple, available in a huge array of sizes and colours, ranging from little buds that are useful for buttonholes all the way to 8cm (3¼in) blooms that are the perfect focal flower for a large table centrepiece. Roses come in a rainbow of colours, as well as dip dyed and with a pearly sheen. You can open this flower up by reflexing the petals to make them even larger and more dramatic (*see* page 36).
- **Zinnia** – These look like little daisies and come in pink, white or yellow. They add cute touches to your designs but the petals are very delicate and break away easily.

TIPS FOR WORKING WITH FOLIAGE

Foliage can be a useful stem to fill in sections of blank space in your designs. You can break off little pieces of foliage from the bottom of the stems to cover your floral foam in a larger design. The remaining stem is much easier to work with when the leaves are focused at the ends: win-win!

Additionally, foliage that drapes, such as eucalyptus nicholii, adds lots of movement to your designs. This kind of foliage is particularly useful to add at the edges of a bouquet to give it a lovely natural shape. Remember, you can mix foliage styles and colours for a naturally foraged look with lots of dimension.

Preserved moss is available year round in a wide array of colours. You can either match your flowers, choose a nice neutral colour or opt for a natural green so that your arrangement appears to be growing straight out of the ground.

Foliage Varieties

Foliage can be useful to add movement and texture to your designs. More and more modern floral designs are omitting foliage altogether to focus on flower-heavy arrangements, but, if used in the right way, foliage can add a wonderful texture and lasts a really long time. There are many preserved foliage varieties available now, but these are my favourites:

- **Beech** – Long, branch-like stems with lots of leaves all the way down. You can break off some of the lower stems to use in other parts of your arrangements. The longer stems are great for meadow-style arrangements and large installations.
- **Eucalyptus baby blue** – Long, thin stems that are covered all the way down with small leaves. This is a very sturdy and straight foliage variety that can be a little more difficult to work with. Comes in green and red-brown as well as in some painted colours.
- **Eucalyptus cinerea** – A classic eucalyptus leaf variety. The leaves vary in size and are small at the end of the stem and larger towards the bottom. The colours range from blue-green to darker shades of green, brown and red.
- **Eucalyptus nicholii** – A feathery leaf that adds lovely movement to your arrangements. Available in red and green.
- **Eucalyptus parvifolia** – Long, branch-like stems with tiny leaves; this foliage adds variety to your designs. Available in green and red, the colours are deep and vivid.
- **Eucalyptus populus** – A draping stem with medium-sized rounded leaves that adds nice natural movement to bouquets. Available in natural red, brown and green, it also comes painted gold and silver for the festive period.
- **Ferns** – I love working with ferns as they add a soft, fluffy, ethereal quality to my designs. These come preserved as well as fresh and in a variety of different painted colours. Fresh ferns can be dried naturally (*see* page 15).
- **Olive** – Very gnarly branches with little straight leaves all at the ends. A lovely Mediterranean foliage that adds a bit of variety.
- **Ruscus** – Long, straight stems with lots of oval-shaped leaves at the ends of the branches. This also comes dried and dyed in lots of different colours, including gold and silver.

Preserved foliage is soft to the touch and has a lovely natural drape. Some varieties are loose and relaxed, while others have a sturdier structure. Choose varieties that work for your colour palette and style of floral arrangement or use multiple types together for a natural look.

Foundational Techniques

In order to begin creating your designs there are a few important technical steps you need to get the hang of. Over the next few pages I will show you how to construct your bouquets in a spiral shape that carefully layers each stem in place – use this technique for all hand-tied bouquets, even arrangements that you place into vases for tables. I will also show you how to split stems of larger-headed flowers and tape these smaller heads onto new stems, and how to wire preserved flower heads, ready for use. Once you conquer these techniques, you will be able to start creating your displays.

The Spiral Technique

The spiral technique is used for all bouquets and fresh floral designs. Using this construction method allows the flowers to be layered up in a perfectly rounded construction. The stems will be added in a methodical way, allowing you to create and modify the design easily as you move along. The end result is a perfectly finished bouquet with clean, tidy stems, which can be enhanced with a beautiful ribbon. If you have created your spiral shape correctly, your bouquet will be able to stand up all on its own. This can be handy if you want to put it down without crushing or flattening your arrangement, or if you want to take a photo of it.

A quick note here before we begin: I am left-handed, so I hold the bouquet in my right hand, leaving my left hand free to select and add each stem to the design. Have a think before you begin on how you would like to work. Do you feel more comfortable holding the bouquet in your dominant hand and working with your other, or would you like to follow my lead here and use your strongest hand to select your stems?

The Method

1. Start your bouquet with two stems of a filler flower such as broom bloom. Cross one stem across the back of the other stem at a 45-degree angle.
2. Add each stem around the bouquet in a circular motion, layering the next one over the last. Hold the stems either just beneath the start of the flowers or below where the stem splits into more branches.
3. Keep turning your bouquet around and add more and more stems at the same angle in the same direction, until you have the beginnings of a nice rounded shape. You can then begin to add different varieties of flowers.
4. Because they are neatly layered onto each other, if you need to remove or add stems you can easily pull one out or add one in without losing your hold on the rest of the flowers. You might need to loosen your grip slightly on the bouquet to do this.
5. Once you have finished your design, you can add floral wire at the hold point – usually about 4–6cm ($1\frac{1}{2}$–$2\frac{1}{4}$in) down from the beginning of the flowers – and cut the stems about 15cm (6in) from the floral bind wire.

Break off stems of broom bloom before you begin so you have nice straight pieces that won't catch on each other. Smaller broken-off pieces can be saved for future designs that need shorter stems, such as table or floor-standing arrangements.

Always work around the arrangement in the same direction. You can move to the left as I do (I'm left handed) or work from the right side if that feels more natural. Experiment with what works best for you.

Stems can be added at different heights right from the beginning of your design, to make the end result feel more natural and relaxed. For a more compact design, add stems closely together at the same height.

I tend to make the stems slightly shorter as I make my way around to the front of the design. This allows for the focal flowers, which are added in the later stages, to sit lower down and be more visible.

Taping Flowers

You can break apart large-headed flowers such as hydrangea to make smaller-headed stems that are more useful. One huge head can be quite overwhelming in a design and using a few smaller heads allows you to use a variety of colours. Hydrangea are also one of the more expensive preserved flowers, so separating them a little means each stem works harder for your design.

You can also apply this taping method to use up little pieces that break off larger blooms so you don't waste anything. Use this same technique for pampas grass plumes; just break off little pieces from the bottom of the plume and tape to discarded stems.

Bold, large-headed blooms such as hydrangea add a lot of focal attraction, so you don't need many to make a real statement. They are a really useful flower that completes a design quickly as they cover a large surface area. Using multiple tones of these flowers within the same design breaks up the mass and gives your arrangement a good dimension.

The Method

1. Break off little pieces of your hydrangea bloom in the size you want to re-stem. You can use one large piece or a few little pieces to create a new bloom.
2. Hold the little stems together and wrap them with floral tape, stretching the tape slightly to allow its sticky side to start working.
3. Once you have wrapped the floral tape a couple of times around the stems, tape a longer cut stem (use one you have saved from a previous cut stem that has a good sturdiness to it) to the bloom you are re-taping. Wrap tape around both stems to secure. You have now created a new stem, ready for use.

I use darker-toned floral tape for darker flowers and white tape for paler flowers. Bear in mind that green is the natural colour for a flower stem, so can be used for any colour flower to look like a real stem.

Breaking off broken stems that hang down means that you clean up your main bloom as well as giving yourself additional little pieces to use for other things. You can collate multiple snippets of these flowers into one larger bloom – consider using different tones together to create even more interest.

Floral tape needs to be 'activated' by stretching it out to make the sticky side work. Once it is sticky, it will attach to itself really well. Floral tape doesn't stick to other things well, so don't use it for taping over anything but floral stems.

Wiring Preserved Flower Heads

Many preserved flowers come in boxes of heads, meaning there is no stem attached to the flower heads. The most common flower head available in this way is the preserved rose. The heads are easy to wire onto a new stem, but they can be quite heavy so need securing well. Once taped to a new stem, you can reflex the petals if you wish (*see* page 36).

The Method

1. Preserved rose heads are sold in protective trays.
2. Take your preserved head out of the protective tray, removing any pins that were there to secure it in place.
3. Use a floral stub wire that is as sturdy as you can get. Create a little rounded loop on one end to stop it coming right through the rose when you insert it.
4. Push the wire through the centre of the rose. You want this to be as central as possible, as this is the hardest part of the rose head and it will ensure that the wire stays in place. Sometimes the rose is very hard in the middle and it can be difficult to get the wire through without it bending. If that happens, just move the wire over a little and let it come out of the side of the centre slightly. Pull the wire through.
5. Choose a discarded stem that is about the same width as the preserved rose stem. Holding it beside the preserved rose stem, start taping it with floral tape, stretching the tape to activate its stickiness.
6. Wrap floral tape all the way down the stem, making sure the top of the stem is strong and well-taped.

Flower heads are quite delicate, so I keep them in these protective trays until I use them. Roses are available in packs singularly or in fours, sixes or eights; smaller roses come in larger packs.

Be gentle with your preserved flower heads as they are expensive, delicate and can be easily damaged. Larger heads are heavier and might need a stronger stem to be attached to. To balance the weight, pick one that is the same size as the stem on your rose.

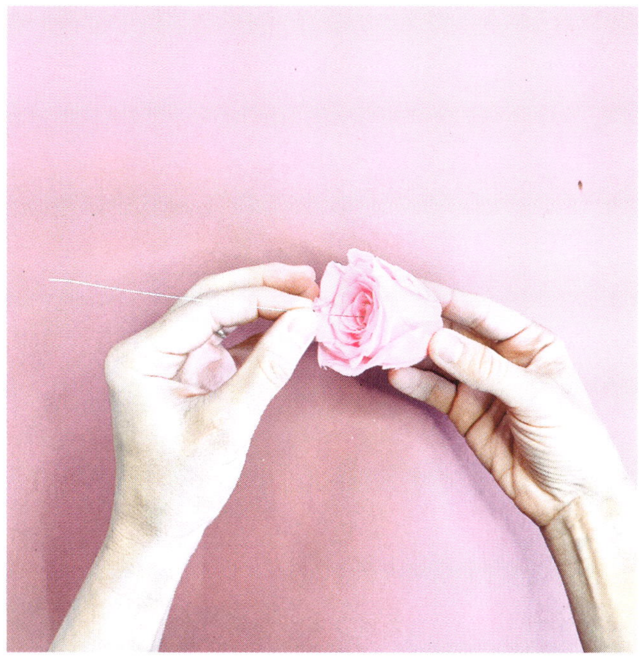

Stub wires can bend very easily so you might need to pull it back out of the rose, straighten it out and start again as you try to push it through the centre. Some roses come with shorter stems that can be difficult to attach; for these, use two stub wires – one at each side – to stabilise the flowers on the stems.

Adding a little loop at the end stops the wire pushing right through the rose. You can then cut the wire in half and use the remainder for another rose, saving you the cost of buying more wire than you need.

Taping the rose to the new stem can be quite challenging and does take a little practice. If it falls off, keep trying.

Wrap the floral tape all the way down the new stem so you can't see where the tape finishes. This makes it appear more like a fresh flower stem.

Reflexing Preserved Rose Heads

Reflexing fresh rose heads is a very popular technique, which adds interest by making your flower heads bigger and more dramatic. It is also possible to use a similar technique to open up preserved rose heads. Make sure you are very gentle with the roses as this technique can sometimes loosen the petals and make the rose collapse. Not all heads allow you to open them up this way, so have a little go and see if the petals open up; if you encounter some resistance, or a petal falls off, just accept this rose head doesn't want to be opened and try another. It's also nice to have a design where some roses are reflexed while others remain closed.

The Method

1. Choose a rose that you have already wired and taped to a new stem (*see* pages 34–35).
2. Start with one of the outermost petals. Pull it down and curve it slightly underneath to almost fold it back.
3. Move around the rose, folding back the whole outer edge of the petals.
4. Move around the flower head to the next layer of petals . After the second row, I like to open up the centre a little by pushing open two or three more petals. This ensures that the opened petals blend in better with the unopened centre of the flower.

Preserved flowers come in a huge array of colours, ranging from deep, inky, dyed tones to bright, light roses. They do fade easily, so keep them out of sunlight while you create your arrangements, unless you want to make the colours softer.

Some rose petals don't like to be reflexed and fall right off. If this happens and you continue trying to pull back the rest of the petals, you are in danger of the rose completely collapsing. If one petal breaks off, leave that rose and try another.

When folding back your petals, you might need to go back over them if they pop back into their original position. Bend them at the middle of the base as they are most shaped in the centre.

Sometimes the centre of the rose is too tightly packed to reflex the petals. Bend the reflexed and non-reflexed parts by gently teasing open the middle, being careful not to tear the petals.

You definitely get more out of each rose as once reflexed, they are larger and more impactful – the flower head increases in size by about 50 per cent, so your final design won't require as many to look beautiful.

PART TWO: CREATE IT

Wedding Flowers

The bouquet is a central part of wedding floral design, but you can use the techniques given in this chapter as a reference for all sorts of designs, including bridal, bridesmaid and vase arrangements for events or the home. In this part of the book, I will give you the base knowledge you need to start designing your wedding flowers with confidence. I have included lots of different colour stories, but you can change these up to suit your needs or match back to your colour palettes. And because all your flowers are dried and preserved, your guests can take home a little something special to remember your perfect day.

When I start designing for a wedding or event, my mind usually settles first on the wedding bouquet. It is often one of the most focal parts of the wedding – the piece that will get the most attention during the day – and I want it to be right, so I spend a good amount of time focusing on its design. On pages 44–56, I will show you the four design shapes and concepts that I most often use in my work – each has a slightly different construction and uses varying floral components. In Part Three (*see* page 135), I will show you how to tie your bouquet with wire and ribbons, how to wrap it with tissue and how to carry your bouquet to show it off optimally.

Once you have designed and created your wedding bouquet (or vase arrangement in the same style), you can move on to the other items needed for the special people in your extended wedding party, which will vary depending on the kind of event you are looking to have. Do you want to go all out by including all of your nearest and dearest or keep things simple by just involving your partner and one or two others? In this chapter, I will give you many ideas for your friends and family, including three stunning bridesmaid bouquet designs (*see* pages 61–72), gorgeous buttonholes for the groomsmen and dads (*see* pages 73–79), and sweet corsages for the mums and grandmothers (*see* pages 80–85).

There is no need to stick to the basics and just create bouquets and buttonholes; there are so many other little finishing touches that will add a real wow factor to your wedding. Later in this part, I will show you how to create flower crowns (*see* page 89), flower girl hoops (*see* page 86) and hair slides (*see* page 93), all adding a little something special to your wedding party's final look.

PLANNING TO A BUDGET

Planning a wedding can be very expensive, and flowers can account for a large part of your spend – even if you are making them yourself. Before you begin designing your wedding flowers, have a think about how much you would like to spend. If you have a larger budget, and plenty of time set aside to create everything, you can max out your florals and create some displays that will take your wedding to the next level. If you are looking to save money, bridesmaid bouquets are cheaper to make by using more affordable stems in simpler designs; the size and scale can also be played with to save on flower costs. Buttonholes can also be very affordable to make, but take a lot of time as they are quite fiddly.

Even a simple elopement wedding can have multiple floral items such as a flower crown, bouquet and buttonhole. Flower girls look adorable with a posy as well as a crown if you really want to maximise your flowers.

Think about which item would work best for each person in your bridal party. Some people prefer something simple, while others want to be part of the dressing up of the day. Consider the clothes that the guest will be wearing; for example, can a silk dress support a pin or corsage or should you opt for a ribbon-tie version?

The Wedding Bouquet

The wedding bouquet is a vital part of creating my concept, so before I begin I think hard about what I want it to look like and which floral components will go into its creation. Choose the design that works best with your aesthetic and bear in mind that you can adapt it for different colour stories or flowers. Think about capturing your entire colour story in that one piece, with other matching floral items perhaps using one or two of the colours each. This allows the wedding bouquet to pull all your items together to create a cohesive story and be the main focal design. Alternatively, every item you make can have the exact same colour story.

The next four tutorials cover the four different styles of bouquet: Rounded Classic (*see* page 44), Asymmetrical Boho (*see* page 48), Relaxed Wildflower (*see* page 52) and Flower-Heavy Design (*see* page 56). These are the basic shapes and styles for you to start with, but they can be adapted if you want to add different flowers or foliage into the mix. Think about using varying heights for your stems and playing with different-sized blooms for more interest. You can also use these methods for various sizes of bouquet – size up for a really dramatic bouquet or down for your bridesmaids or flower girls. Remember to use your spiral technique (*see* page 30) when creating your bouquet (you can use this even if you are making a vase of flowers at home or a bouquet as a gift for a friend).

There are many things that need to be considered to create a perfect bouquet. You can look back to Part One for all the tips and tricks that should go into your research, but as a quick recap you need to think about the style, the colours and the shape before you begin. By now you should have decided on which flowers you would like to focus on, the colours you would like to use and the specific items you would like to make. Once you have decided which of the four designs to create, the rest of your floral items can match back to this style – you have created your concept!

Use the most beautiful flowers to ensure that your bridal bouquets stand out. They will probably be the most photographed and impactful items that you'll create.

Rounded Classic

The most useful design to master for bouquets is the rounded classic. This can be adapted for so many different styles, whether you want something romantic, classic and contemporary – think an even distribution of roses and foliage – or something bolder, with brightly coloured dried flowers and foliage.

Modern floral designs tend to be less regimented and have a softer, more relaxed feel, which is the style I refer to the most in my work. My rounded designs are still relaxed and slightly wild as I don't favour something that is too neat or compact. When you develop your style, you can adapt this design to be tighter and more compact or bigger and wilder – whichever works best with your ideas and themes.

The Method

1. Begin by taking two or three stems of your first filler flower – I am using dried broom bloom and dried gypsophila because both are great flowers to fill in and add bulk. This will give your bouquet a good structure and hold all the other stems in place well. Cross one stem across the back of another to form an X (*see* the spiral technique on page 30).
2. After creating the initial shape, I like to add in some foliage to break up the dried stems. Don't wait too long to add your foliage; otherwise you will end up with a dense plain section in the middle of your bouquet.
3. Next, I add some dried flowers. This is a good time to add any smaller-headed blooms such as statice or helichrysum, but in this design I add lepidium and phalaris. Keep turning your bouquet so that you add flowers and foliage all around (including to the back of the design). Aim for a rounded shape that can be enjoyed from all angles.
4. I now start to add my focal blooms. These could be roses, hydrangea or large-bloomed dried flowers such as palm cups. Here I use three different shades of roses in slightly different sizes. I add these at varying heights all around the bouquet, focusing the lowest at the front of the design.
5. Continue to add foliage and dried flowers in layers as you make your way around the bouquet.
6. Add in any lighter, fluffier stems such as bunny tails or pampas grasses. Pampas grass can be separated from its stem and taped onto smaller stems (*see* page 32) to be used in smaller quantities. Sometimes it is necessary to relax your hold on the bouquet and feed one or two stems into the middle of your design; this is why the spiral technique is so important as it allows us to work in and out of the bouquet when needed.
7. Give your bouquet its last few checks by pushing down or pulling up stems to adjust their height. Ensure your shape is as you want it by adding a few fluffier or more open stems such as pampas, ferns or soft foliage (this is also a great way to hide any of the mechanics such as floral taping). Check that all sides are beautiful (don't forget the back).
8. Tie your bouquet with floral wire at the break point, about 4–6cm (1½–2¼in) from the start of the flowers.
9. Cut your stems with sharp secateurs. I like to cut the stems about 15cm (6in) from the floral bind wire.

STEMS USED IN THIS DESIGN

This design has a soft, muted colour palette with a touch of peach. I used two different types of foliage and natural pampas grass. Because this bouquet is such a classic design it would work for any season, but it would look completely different with an alternative colour palette and different flowers.

- **Base dried flowers** – Dried broom bloom and dried gypsophila to help you start your shape off.
- **Large focal flowers** – Preserved roses in three colours.
- **Foliage** – Preserved eucalyptus cinerea and preserved eucalyptus parfivolia.
- **Selection of dried flowers and grasses** – Including dried phalaris, dried oats, dried lepidium, dried ferns and dried pampas grass.

The bridal bouquet can help to set the tone for the entire floral design of your wedding. You can centre your entire colour story around it.

Use a selection of stems that complement each other well – different scales of flower heads and shades of colour within a complementary palette. In this design I have used a selection of ivory, natural green and peach dried stems with preserved roses in three different shades. Using more than one type of foliage adds depth to your design.

Start your bouquet with two to three crossed stems, which will begin its important spiral base. Crossing the stems helps you start the spiral technique, which will allow you to add stems in an orderly way. Use different types of flowers to give a little variation and make your bouquet centre more open and loftier.

Adding some larger stems such as eucalyptus helps to create shape and add interest. Eucalyptus comes in many varieties, so choose the type you like or mix a few varieties for a more dynamic look (*see* eucalyptus varieties on page 28).

Longer-stemmed blooms such as lepidium add interest to your bouquet and help create varying heights. Lepidium is a lovely stem to add more natural green tones; using different green dried flowers gives more of a foliage-heavy look but adds structure to your design.

The biggest flowers add volume, shape and the most drama. Large-headed flowers are usually preserved, meaning they are soft to the touch, but there are a few varieties that have large heads, such as achillea, protea, dried hydrangea and palm cups. Palm cups are available in their natural colour, bleached white or dyed in a variety of amazing shades.

Feed in pampas stems where you need them – keep trying different places until you find the most appealing place to put them. Think about whether you want to have a lot of pampas grass for a dramatic, bohemian-style bouquet or little touches to give a romantic, fluffy appearance.

You can cut stems shorter for smaller bouquets, such as flower girl posies, or keep the stems longer for a more dramatic look. Bouquets with lots of long pampas look really nice with longer stems, so don't cut them too short – you can't put it back once it's been cut!

Asymmetrical Boho

Not all bouquets are designed to be enjoyed from all angles. I am now going to show you how to create a bouquet in an asymmetrical shape, with longer stems on one side. Because of its shape, this style of bouquet needs to be carried across the body – held slightly forward facing at an angle – so it does not need to be designed in a completely circular way. We can therefore focus our flowers to the side and front for the biggest impact.

This modern design has become popular since pampas grass has begun trending again for weddings – the longer focal stems of the grass create the shape. You could also use long stems of PeeGee hydrangea, long foliage stems or a bunch of bunny tails at one side. Play around with your stems by holding them roughly into shape to see if you like their proportions before you begin.

STEMS USED IN THIS DESIGN

This is a pale and pretty colour palette with a touch of dark burgundy to give it the edge that I'm always looking for with my designs – something a little unexpected. The hydrangea give this bouquet a gorgeous structure and the pampas grasses help me achieve the asymmetrical shape I'm looking for. The colour palette would be stunning for a winter wedding, but adding in a little pink or an unexpected hint of something bright would give this bouquet a spring or summer feel.

- **Base dried flowers** – A combination of dried broom bloom and preserved gypsophila.
- **Main focal blooms** – Two shades of preserved hydrangea.
- **Foliage** – Preserved red eucalyptus populus.
- **Selection of dried grasses and flowers** – I chose dried bunny tails, dried oats, dried thistles, dried nigella, preserved craspedia and dried pampas grass.

The Method

1. Begin with the spiral technique (*see* page 30), using three or four stems of broom bloom. A rounded starting point for this design will give the bouquet a good structure.
2. Add in some of your dried flowers and grasses. These will give the bouquet a good shape and add some interest to the centre of the design. Save some for after you have added your main flowers, as we will continue to add everything in layers.
3. Start adding in your focal flowers. Begin with hydrangea, as these flowers have extra-large blooms that will create your shape for you (*see* page 33 for how to separate and tape your hydrangea blooms). You can begin by adding two or three to help get the shape you want – think about putting them in at different heights to give your bouquet more interest. Don't forget to add some at the back of your design to ensure a nice round shape.
4. Add in two or three palm leaves – two to one side of the bouquet and one towards the back in the middle. I like to use these to create impact so I want them grouped together towards one side (remember you will be adding pampas or something longer stemmed to the other side of the bouquet). Place these at different heights, which will look more impactful.
5. Keep adding layers of broom bloom, dried flowers and grasses in the spiral method to fill out your shape. Think about your layering to ensure interesting stems are placed throughout the design.
6. Add two or three stems of pampas grass on the opposite side to the palm leaves. Leave these stems long and dramatic. You have now created your asymmetrical shape.
7. Turn your bouquet around and add broom bloom and dried flowers and grasses to the back to 'round out' the arrangement. You might need to add one more head of hydrangea here to make a nice shape –aim for a rounded shape with long strands of pampas grass on one side.
8. Add some flowers that have movement, such as gypsophila or wheat, to the sides of the bouquet for a more relaxed feel.
9. Tie your bouquet with floral wire and cut the stems.

Asymmetrical bouquets are a modern take on more classic shapes, often featuring pampas grasses, that need to be held across the body rather than centrally. Pampas grass comes in a variety of shades, from deep dyed colours to lightly dyed, natural-looking tones as well as a completely natural beige. All natural stems vary slightly in their tones so make sure you have seen them in person before you create your colour palettes.

Focal hydrangeas in different shades create a beautiful contrast with natural pampas grasses. Using more than one colour of hydrangea in your bouquet adds something unexpected for a more dynamic look. Even two tones of the same colour family will make your bouquet look much more natural and emulate fresh flowers more closely.

Begin your design with three or four stems placed at 45-degree angles. Consider using a couple of colours to add further interest to your bouquet – broom bloom is a lovely flower that comes in a multitude of colours, from bleached white all the way to dark black. It is also available as a preserved stem, but I find it lacks structure and doesn't have the same longevity.

I love to add dried stems in groups for an asymmetrical design. Add in groups of thistles together or groups of wheat all at one side to make the design bolder and more graphic.

Larger blooms help us create a rounded shape before we add our longer-stemmed pampas. With a dramatic and bold design, it will always look better to use a few stems of a large flower rather than lots of stems of smaller flowers.

Pampas grasses and ruscus create height and asymmetry, but you could use other longer stems if you want a cleaner look. Any flower with longer stems would work well, such as a PeeGee hydrangea (a long, shaped version of the standard hydrangea) or large palm leaves or palm cups. Alternatively, you can group smaller-headed flowers together in a bunch to emulate the appearance of one large flower.

Relaxed Wildflower

Wildflower-style bouquets can be designed with any colour scheme and selection of dried flowers. This relaxed style of bouquet uses only dried flowers and grasses – no foliage or large blooms. It is not tightly made but has lots of different heights and levels, so it appears to have been assembled by gathering these flowers and grasses in your garden or along hedgerows, and roughly assembling them together for a slightly wild, natural and foraged look.

Smaller-headed flowers work best, such as rhodanthe, helichrysum, bunny tails, statice, wheat and oats. Pepper in lots of grasses and even ferns for a wild, relaxed look. Most of the flowers are added evenly, not in groups, so the design has a uniform appearance. I added some ferns around the edges of the bouquet, but otherwise the flowers are all mixed together.

STEMS USED IN THIS DESIGN

This bright and beautiful bouquet is a combination of mostly dried flowers and grasses, layered up so that the flowers are placed throughout – rather than focusing on any particular stem at either side of the bouquet – giving a lovely even appearance. I like to place stems at varying heights so the overall look is very relaxed and appears like just-picked wildflowers.

- **Base dried flowers** – A mixture of dried broom bloom and preserved gypsophila.
- **Main focal blooms** – I used one slightly larger flower type, dried achillea, which is used throughout, and not placed, for an even, blended appearance.
- **Selection of dried grasses and flowers** – The rest of the design is made up entirely with dried grasses and flowers including dried rhodanthe, dried phalaris, dried oats, dried ruscus, dried ferns, dried lepidium and dried feather grass.

The Method

1. Begin with your spiral technique (*see* page 30). Use three or four stems of your base dried flowers, remembering to cross them over one another and keep moving around in the same direction. For this design I like to use a combination of broom bloom, which is drier and denser, and preserved gypsophila, which is softer and more open. This ensures the bouquet remains light and lofty while still having plenty of movement.
2. I start to add in some of my favourite dried stems such as rhodante and oats. There can be a lot of dried, shrivelled leaves on rhodante stems – it can be helpful to remove these before you begin – then add the rhodante stems in bunches together. This is less laborious and also gives a more emotional look as the rhodante have fine stems that naturally sit at different heights in an organic way.
3. Next, add a few larger-headed flowers such as achillea. These would be the largest-headed stems I would use for this design. They add pops of solid colour to the overall look but your eye isn't drawn to them too much, especially as you pepper them throughout.
4. Keep moving your bouquet around, layering up the same flowers – more rhodante, more dried grasses, touches of fluffy grass and lots of wheat and oats.
5. Add gypsophila at different heights and around the sides, as well as a touch of fern. This will give the bouquet an ethereal quality.
6. Tie with floral wire and cut your stems with sharp secateurs.

Wildflower bouquets are a wonderful way to add colour to a wedding. Here I use many different tones of the same palette to create a gorgeous colour story. This bouquet uses lots of different varieties within the same colour family – all the tones are warm with lots of pinks and oranges. You could create the same bouquet using the whole spectrum of colour in a rainbow appearance too.

This is a rainbow-inspired colour palette using small-headed stems such as rhodanthe, gypsophila, lepidium and wheat. Using smaller stems allows for a more blended appearance with an overall even look; no one flower stands out on its own but it is nice to have one or two more dynamic flowers that add depth to your design. Here I used achillea and ruscus for a little more impact.

Neon-pink gypsophila makes a colourful base for this design, which is less dense than broom bloom on its own. Gypsophila is available dried or preserved, and both work well in bouquets. The preserved stems tend to have bigger flowers so they look a little more impressive within the bouquet, but dried versions add a little more depth than just using broom bloom or something with a smaller head. You can dry your own gypsophila by hanging it upside down.

Nigella at varying heights adds drama and shows off interesting stems. This nigella was dried naturally by hanging it upside down for a few weeks. It has a lovely natural purple hue, which adds whimsy to the bouquet.

Layer your stems evenly throughout your design for a natural, foraged look. Wildflower foraged-style bouquets are a popular design, especially for the summer months, as they are a wonderful way to achieve a bright, colourful look. Imagine finishing this bouquet with colourful ribbons.

Ferns are a wonderful flower that you can dry yourself. They come in a huge variety of shades, and the colour is well retained after drying. Ferns add a little fluffiness without the need for pampas grasses, but beware, they do shed quite a bit.

Flower-Heavy Design

Flower-heavy designs are exactly that – arrangements created with all flowers, no foliage. With this style, I like to use a lot of large-headed stems such as roses and hydrangea. I still begin by using a few stems of dried flowers such as broom bloom to help achieve the shape and make the bouquet nice and sturdy. This is a bold design, so I like to use bold colours such as clashing reds and pinks, but it works equally well in all white or pale pastels. As with all of my designs, I like to play with proportion and position the stems at varying heights to show off each impactful flower.

The Method

1. Begin with the spiral technique (*see* page 30), using three or four stems of broom bloom. Use one or two stems of gypsophila to open up the centre of the design. Remember to cross each stem over one another and keep moving around in the same direction.
2. Add in groups of five or six stems of dried flowers at a time as you make your way around the bouquet. Use dried phalaris to add some interest into the centre of the bouquet before layering in the larger blooms.
3. Start adding the focal blooms, which make up the main part of this design. A few large heads of hydrangea allow me to quickly create a rounded shape. Add some achillea stems at varying heights too. Don't worry too much about the height you place them in – you can easily push them up or down once you get closer to finishing your bouquet.
4. Add your most beautiful flowers now – your roses. Again, place these at different heights and use various shades in different places; for example, two pinks on one side and a red on the other. Keep turning the bouquet around to make sure that there are flowers on all sides, even the back, saving your favourite and most beautiful stems to be placed towards the front (*see* page 36 for how to reflex roses, which will add even more drama to your bouquet design).
5. Now you are nearing the end of your creation, add in stems that have more movement. Lots of gypsophila and touches of fluffy pampas are placed around the sides, covering any rose stems that have been taped and ensuring the bouquet is loose, has a relaxed feeling and is not too compact.
6. Add a few bunny tails at varying heights – less is more; don't be tempted to add too many. Bunny tails add whimsy to your design as they move beautifully. I add eight or nine through the arrangement in groups of three, ensuring there are one or two at the back.
7. Add your floral wire and cut your stems with sharp secateurs.

STEMS USED IN THIS DESIGN

This graphic and bold design is made with mostly preserved flowers, so it feels quite soft and natural. The preserved gypsophila adds a lovely movement as it is placed primarily around the edges. Further boldness comes from the intense colour palette of pinks and reds. The larger flowers are focused to the centre of the design, with one or two choice stems adding height at either side.

- **Base dried flowers** – A combination of dried broom bloom and preserved gypsophila.
- **Bold large-headed preserved blooms** – Hydrangea and roses.
- **Dried grasses and flowers** – A few choice dried stems such as achillea (also a large-headed flower, but this one is dried), bunny tails and touches of pampas grass.

Bold colour palettes add further intensity to a flower-heavy bouquet that uses mostly preserved flowers. This bouquet has two main colours, but in order to make it look natural and create more depth, I use lots of different shades within them. Pink ranges from the palest tones all the way to a hot neon shade and the red comes in deeper as well as brighter shades.

Keeping your colour palette focused to two colours in multiple shades can create a dynamic look, but think about the different scales of the flowers – here ranging from tiny bunny tail heads all the way to large preserved hydrangea blooms. Preserved roses are available in many sizes, varieties and colours so play around with proportion and colour.

Preserved gypsophila mixed with broom bloom creates the perfect base layer. Using pops of bold neon colour makes sure this design is really impactful.

Add dried flowers in little bunches to save time. You can prep your flowers in piles of each variety before you begin, ensuring that you are ready to add handfuls at a time. Some flowers come with loose leaves that need removing or broken stems that need to be filtered out.

Large focal flowers such as hydrangea create drama. If you are using multiple shades, make sure you break these up throughout the design, unless you are intentionally grouping colours together in bold blocks. The colour-blocked appearance only works well when it is obvious.

Roses make this design stand out. Add them at different heights and in varying scales for the best look. Preserved roses are commonly available in sizes ranging from tiny buds through to 7–8cm (2¾–3¼in) blooms.

Focus your gypsophila at the edges to soften your bouquet shape. I am always striving for as much movement as possible in my designs to ensure that I am emulating the appearance of fresh flowers as much as possible. Adding flowers with lots of natural movement at the edges of my bouquets ensures I get the most movement possible with the dried stems.

Cut your stems for a clean finish – they should be cut straight on a bouquet, not angled. It is worth investing in a pair of good-quality secateurs as some stems are thick and tough. This will make your making days much easier; in addition, you will get a clean edge that looks much nicer.

Consider the colour of your ribbons when finishing your bouquets. Adding a contrast ribbon can elevate your design and add something special, or you can choose one of the colours within the bouquet to highlight.

Bridesmaid Bouquets

In the following pages you will find three different bridesmaid bouquet designs, starting with the most expensive to produce, the Small Bridesmaid Bouquet – basically a smaller version of the wedding bouquet. I will then show you the much simpler Bridesmaid Posy (*see* page 65) and introduce you to the Asymmetrical Pampas Bouquet (*see* page 69), which are small but dramatic because of their use of long pampas stems.

In my opinion, the best design to create for your bridesmaids is something that resembles your own bouquet. This ensures that the bridal party looks cohesive and creates a lovely story, with the flowers being a focal part of that. You could create this in a colour story that works with your wedding bouquet or you could make your bridesmaid bouquets slightly different in colour; for example, if your bouquet is a collection of pastel tones, the bridesmaid arrangements could all be pastel pink.

STEMS USED IN THIS DESIGN

This is a bold statement colour palette that is ideal for a winter wedding. Deep tones of burgundy and red are offset with the palest sand roses and graphic black palm leaves. Note all the different shades that make up this colour palette and give a nod to the season.

- **Base dried flower** – Dried broom bloom.
- **Large focal flowers** – Preserved roses in two colours and preserved hydrangea in burgundy.
- **Foliage** – Eucalyptus parvifolia and baby eucalyptus with brown beech leaves, palm leaves and pampas grass.

Small Bridesmaid Bouquet

Here I show you how to create a small version of the wedding bouquet in a different style to those I have already shown you, giving you another option to pick from for your larger bouquet too. This is a flower-heavy design, but it does feature one or two graphic foliage stems. You can also refer back to the previous wedding bouquets on pages 44–56 and make smaller versions of those if you prefer.

The Method

1. Begin by taking two or three stems of your first filler flower – I use dried broom bloom to give this bouquet a good structure and hold all the other stems in place well. Take one stem and cross the next stem across the back at a 45-degree angle, using the spiral technique (*see* page 30).
2. Add in stems of different foliage to make sure that the foliage runs throughout the design.
3. This bouquet is all about the focal blooms, so now add one of your hydrangea and two or three preserved roses. Start to add some palm leaves to add a hard contrast to the soft preserved flowers.
4. Continue layering dried flowers and foliage, and begin to add touches of pampas grass to soften everything. Remember to add these stems at a 45-degree angle, continually turning the bouquet around to make sure the shape remains rounded and the stems are added evenly.
5. Add one or two hydrangea flowers at the side and back to fill out the bouquet. You will also need to add broom bloom and some foliage to the back to ensure a nice rounded shape.
6. Do one last check. Maybe add some more pampas grass and push the stems up and down until you like the finished result.
7. Tie your bouquet with floral bind wire about 4–5cm (1¾–2in) down from the start of your flowers.
8. Cut your stems with sharp secateurs. You might want to cut these a little shorter than your wedding bouquet depending on the age of your bridesmaids; younger bridesmaids might need shorter stems.

These smaller-scale versions of the wedding bouquet still feature all the flowers from the larger bouquet. This is the costliest design for bridesmaids, which amplifies the floral colour story, but you could opt for something simpler if you prefer.

I start all my bouquets with a few stems of a filler flower such as broom bloom as it provides a good structure for the design. This bouquet also has foliage running throughout.

Using palm leaves is a nice way of adding varying heights to your bouquets. They need to be added towards the middle of the design so they stay in position well; adding at the outer edges can be unstable.

Using a variety of preserved flowers in a selection of colours really adds to the final design. Hydrangeas help to round out the shape of the bouquet well as they are such a large-headed flower.

Adding pampas at the final stages adds a lovely movement and softens the contrasting colour scheme on this design. As dried flowers have a sturdier structure than fresh flowers, I am always striving for as natural a shape and movement as possible.

The Bridesmaid Posy is a smaller-scale design that is perfect for younger bridesmaids or flower girls. It also offers a cost-saving solution for adult bridesmaids as it uses fewer stems than a standard bridesmaid bouquet but still matches the floral theme.

Bridesmaid Posy

This simple, timeless and versatile posy can be used to complement most wedding bouquets that feature a little foliage. For flower-heavy arrangements, you can refer to the previous design; for wildflower-style designs, you can use this tutorial as a guide but just eliminate the foliage and use more dried stems.

This bouquet is the perfect little addition for your bridal party because it is a pared-back version that matches the rest of the flowers in your collection, making it super simple and quick to make. It can also be reused in little jam jars on your tables after the ceremony to make the most out of your flowers.

The Method

1. Begin with dried broom bloom and a touch of dried gypsophila to ensure that your posy is open and relaxed in its feel - not too dense. Remember to cross your stems over as you follow the spiral technique (*see* page 30).
2. Add a few stems of eucalyptus early on, so your design will have this running throughout, avoiding a blank section in the middle. This is an evenly blended floral design that looks nicest with all the different stems added throughout it.
3. Start adding dried stems all the way around your design. As this is a really small bouquet, make sure the dried stems run throughout so it still has a lot of interest and variation. Add some longer stems of gypsophila to give the bouquet some height difference.
4. Keep layering more and more stems, finally adding in a few bunny tails, I used seven or eight for this bouquet, and some stems of pampas for a little bit of fluff.
5. Tie your bouquet with floral bind wire and cut your stems.

STEMS USED IN THIS DESIGN

This simple design is in a lovely natural colour palette with a touch of pale pink, but you could use any colour that matches back to the rest of your flowers.

- **Base dried flowers** – Dried broom bloom with a few touches of pink dried gypsophila.
- **Touches of foliage** – Two different eucalyptus stems: parfivolia and cinerea.
- **Dried grasses and flowers** – I used lepidium, wheat and phalaris.

The base stems are a mix of different textures and colours, ensuring lots of interest is added right from the beginning of the design. Tonal colours are used for a subtle look.

Adding foliage early on in the design phase gives a nice even distribution of flowers to foliage. As this design is so simple, it is important to pay special attention to the construction because there aren't many different stems to work with.

Adding in taller lengths of some of the flowers gives this bouquet lots of drama. Here I used longer lengths of gypsophila and kept my wheat stems nice and long. I added wheat all the way through the design as it is a stem with a lot of natural movement.

Adding little pieces of pampas grass that I taped onto discarded stems throughout the design adds a softness to the bouquet and puffs out the shape to make it more rounded.

This simple design can be reused in little jars on the tables for your wedding breakfast. This not only makes the most use out of them but also makes sure they are kept safe for the bridesmaids to take home after the wedding.

Asymmetrical bridesmaid bouquets with long stems of pampas grass are a perfect pairing to any boho bouquet. For such small bouquets, they have so much drama and work well in any colour combination.

Asymmetrical Pampas Bouquet

This design is a little different to your usual bridesmaid bouquet. Pampas grass gives it a really unusual look, as does the length of the stems – the bouquet itself is quite small, but the long stems make it appear more special. I use one protea in this design, which looks stunning as they are such large-headed blooms. You can make this with or without the foliage depending on the look you want to achieve.

These bouquets make perfect table centrepieces that you can place into little bottle vases after your ceremony – once you add your bouquets to the bottles, tie the ribbons into bows for an added touch. Don't use so many flowers that the stems don't fit into the bottles – check the bottle openings before you finish your bouquet.

The Method

1. Begin your bouquet with three or four stems of broom bloom – use two colours to give more interest to the design. Layer them using the spiral technique (*see* page 30) so you can begin to get your rounded shape quickly.
2. As this is a really small bouquet, we need to start adding our focal flowers quickly. Add one open protea flower, some wheat and one stem of dried delphinium. Remove the dried green parts to the delphinium before you add it, as they shed easily and don't look very appealing.
3. Add in some stems of foliage and one long stem of pampas, so you can see how the shape is taking hold.
4. Complete your design with more dried stems, some foliage to frame the edges and a little more pampas grass. Don't forget to add some broom bloom and dried flowers to the back of the design to make it look more finished.
5. Tie your bouquet with floral bind wire and cut your stems, leaving them longer than usual to add a little more drama.

STEMS USED IN THIS DESIGN

This design is in a gorgeous autumnal colour palette with lots of different tones of red, brown and green. The natural pampas tones beautifully with the rest of the bouquet and softens the harder foliage colours.

- **Base dried flowers** – Dried broom bloom in two colours.
- **Touches of foliage** – Brown eucalyptus and green eucalyptus populus.
- **Dried grasses and flowers** – Dried open protea flower, dried delphinium, dried wheat and pampas grass.

Using two contrasting tones of broom bloom means that we don't need to worry about breaking up large sections of filler flowers – the colour contrast does this for us.

Add your strongest, most dramatic focal flowers at the front of the design where they can be seen easily. A small bouquet only needs one or two focal flowers to look beautiful.

Sometimes you need to add flowers in the middle of the bouquet to break up a section or give height. Just loosen your hold on the stems and feed additional stems in where needed.

Adding one or two stems of pampas and keeping the stems really long is the most important part of this design. The long stems balance the shape of the whole bouquet.

Experiment with ribbons of different widths. Smaller bouquets and posies look nice with skinnier ribbons, but you might want to consider using more of them or leaving their length longer.

Buttonholes

It's about time we focused a little attention on the boys in the wedding party. Buttonholes are really simple and easy to make, but they are time-consuming if you have a lot to make so do ensure you allow enough time to create them. They are a little fiddly too, so are not something you can rush. I'm going to show you three lovely ideas: a simple buttonhole (perfect for the groomsmen), a more elaborate buttonhole (ideal for the groom) and a pocket meadow design (a fun idea for making things a little different).

Simple Groomsmen's Buttonhole

You can use this method for all buttonholes – just switch out the stems and colours to match the rest of the wedding flowers. Buttonholes work best with smaller-headed flowers and maybe one focal flower. Try to source roses that are a little smaller to avoid the buttonhole getting too weighty and not sitting nicely on the jacket.

The Method

1. Start your buttonhole with two or three short stems of dried broom bloom and dried gypsophila. Try to spiral them (*see* page 30) as though this is a tiny version of a bouquet because this will keep the stems orderly and ensure the finished result is neat.
2. On a buttonhole, smaller flowers look best positioned in groups of three. Add a group of three stems at different heights.
3. Now add some little pieces of foliage and one longer stem of lepidium at the back. Place your dried stems at different heights.
4. Finally, add a stem of wheat on one side to increase the width of your buttonhole.
5. Tie with floral bind wire and cut your stems about 4cm (1¾in) from the wire.

STEMS USED IN THIS DESIGN

The groomsmen's buttonholes feature just a few strands of dried flowers in a simple, timeless and sophisticated colour story.

- **Base dried flowers** – Dried broom bloom and dried gypsophila.
- **Focal dried flowers** – Dried phalaris, dried wheat and dried lepidium.
- **Foliage** – A couple of stems of classic baby eucalyptus and eucalyptus nicholii.

OPPOSITE: Buttonholes, also known as *boutonnieres*, are made to match the rest of the flowers you design. I use only a few flower varieties, ideally with smaller-headed blooms that are easier to work with.

Buttonholes need two pins to help them stay straight on a jacket or shirt. They work best when they don't get too heavy. Make sure the shape is quite triangular and not too thin, as it will get lost on a jacket.

Think of your buttonhole as a miniature bouquet. Start the design with a few pieces of a filler flower to give it a nice structure.

As buttonholes are so small, I use fine-stemmed flowers for this.

Using little stems of foliage removed from longer stems for other designs means that nothing is wasted.

Using finer, more delicate flowers means that the stems don't get too bulky. This is essential for buttonholes as the stems are visible when the item is worn.

Groom's Buttonhole

This classic design is basically the same as the Simple Groomsmen's Buttonhole (*see* the method on page 73) with one larger focal flower at the front. You could substitute the rose for a large dried flower such as achillea or two or three helichrysum.

Adding Ribbon to Your Buttonhole

You can finish your buttonhole in a number of ways, but the general idea is to cover the floral bind wire with something to match back to your bouquets and wedding colour story. You can either finish with some rustic hessian, tie them with ribbon or string in a little knot, or add a strip of satin ribbon. I am going to show you how to finish cleanly with glue and ribbon, but you could also tie this if you don't mind the knot showing. Knots look best with narrower ribbon, and remember to cut the ends at a 45-degree angle so they don't fray easily.

For a super-special buttonhole, add a preserved rose. The smaller the rose the better, as they get quite heavy and are hard to secure to a jacket without hanging off at an angle.

1. Once your buttonhole is finished with floral bind wire and the stems are cut, you can select your ribbon choice – here I am using a simple ivory satin ribbon. Cut the end of the ribbon so it has a straight edge. Add a little glue to this edge and start wrapping the ribbon from the back of the buttonhole.
2. Wrap the ribbon around two or three times to a desired height and cut the end straight with some sharp scissors. Measure the length so that the end will finish on the back of the buttonhole.
3. Add some glue neatly to the end of the ribbon and press it firmly. Hold it in place for a few seconds to make sure it has stuck.
4. Once the glue is dry and you are happy with the appearance, you can add two pins to the back of the ribbon. These will be used to attach the buttonhole to the shirt or jacket.

STEMS USED IN THIS DESIGN

To make your groom's buttonhole a little more special, I add a preserved rose. This adds a little drama, while keeping the colour palette classic.

- **Base dried flowers** – Dried broom bloom and dried gypsophila.
- **Focal dried flowers** – Dried phalaris, dried wheat and dried lepidium.
- **Dried flower** – One preserved rose.
- **Foliage** – A couple of stems of classic baby eucalyptus and eucalyptus nicholii.

You can complete your buttonhole with all sorts of different finishings such as satin ribbons, string, hessian, organza or fabric strips, either tied in knots, with bows or attached cleanly with glue.

Sometimes glue can transfer onto the outer edge of the ribbon; once dried, this can be peeled off easily.

Using a clear liquid glue means that you can easily control where it goes and it won't be seen if it spills on to the outer edges of your ribbon.

I use pearl-headed pins as they are very simple, but you can get pins with all sorts of ends in different colours or metal finishes. They are readily available online or in haberdashery shops.

Pocket Meadow

The cutest little pop of florals made on a ribbon-wrapped card to slip into your jacket pocket; you can make these using all kinds of flowers and foliage to match the rest of your designs. You can even add fluffy pampas or metallic touches for a more dramatic look. The Pocket Meadow is a nice touch if you are a same-sex couple and you want to look a little more special than the rest of your wedding party, or if you have a male member of the bridal party who would like to stand out from the other groomsmen.

The Method

1. Cut a piece of card the right size to fit into a breast pocket on a jacket. You should check the pocket size dimensions for the exact size needed, ensuring that you cut the card slightly smaller than the opening to allow for the ribbon. This one is approximately 10cm (4in) tall and 8cm (3¼in) wide.
2. Wrap the card with ribbon. You can secure the start of the ribbon with a piece of sticky tape and cover that with one round of the ribbon. Once you have covered the whole card, cut a nice clean straight edge on the ribbon and glue it down.
3. Apply a 3cm (1¼in) strip of glue on the top edge of your ribboned card. Do this on the same side as the end of the ribbon so that you can cover it with your flowers.
4. Start applying your flowers to the ribbon card over the glue. I start with larger leaves here to cover the top edge. If you need to add more glue once they are stuck down, do this now.
5. Next, stick little pieces of broom bloom on top of the leaves, always working from the centre out to the edges.
6. Add some smaller stems and leaves on top. Keep layering up your chosen stems.
7. Once you are happy with your base layer, you can glue on a preserved rose or large-bloomed flower in the middle. Finally, add a little piece of hydrangea to cover all the stems in the centre.

ITEMS USED IN THIS DESIGN

The Pocket Meadows are in a stunning palette of deep burgundy, brown, pale latte-coloured roses and preserved foliage in a mixture of tones. These colours are perfect for a winter wedding but with the touches of black they would work well for a more gothic-style wedding, whatever the season.

- **Decorations** – A piece of card and ribbon for the base.
- **Preserved foliage** – Preserved beech leaves and preserved eucalyptus parvifolia.
- **Base dried flower** – Dried broom bloom.
- **Preserved flowers** – Preserved rose and preserved hydrangea pieces.

Pocket Meadows are a lovely way to amplify the floral look for anyone wearing a jacket. They are bigger and more dramatic than a regular buttonhole.

Since you are covering your base with ribbon, you only need to use a bit of discarded card or something similar. You can use ribbon, hessian or fabric to cover your base; just make sure it isn't too sheer so the card is hidden.

Using large leaves covers a bigger area and can provide a nice base. This is also a good way to use leaves you have discarded from longer stems to avoid wasting anything.

Always work from the middle out to the edge and layer up a variety of flowers and foliage for a more eclectic and natural look.

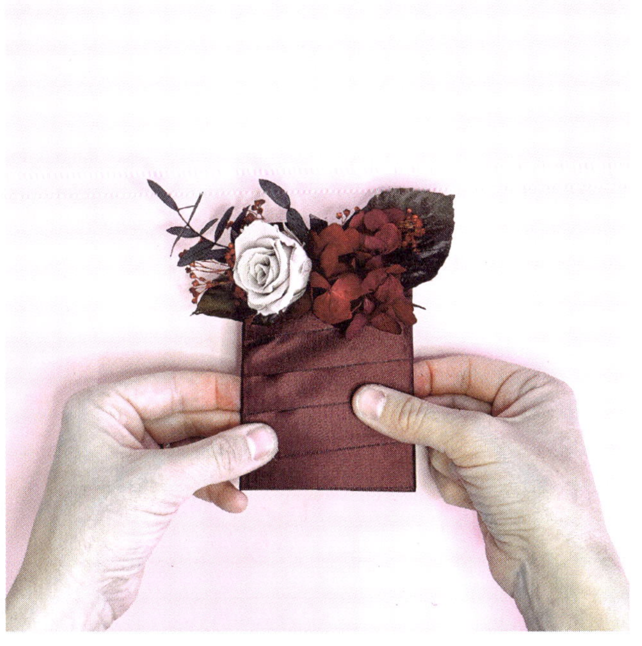

Using one or two larger-headed flowers in the middle of your design helps to cover up the stems of the base layers of flowers. I like to use hydrangea pieces here as they are large but light and will glue easily on to the centre.

Corsages and Accessories

Buttonholes are not saved solely for the menfolk. Now that weddings are becoming more unconventional, there is often a need for a little something floral for the mums and grandmas. First, we look at corsages – I will show you how to make something more feminine for the mums to pin on (*see* page 82), followed by an alternative idea if pinning does not work with their outfit choice: the Ribbon-Tie Corsage (*see* page 84).

Alternatively, floral hoops (*see* page 86) look lovely when carried by a flower girl or can be a different idea for adult bridesmaids. Or, for something different, why not embellish the hair with a beautiful floral display? I will show you how to create gorgeous flower crowns (*see* page 89) and hair slides (*see* page 93), that are guaranteed to bring a smile to the big day.

Flower crowns take a long time to make as they are very fiddly. Make sure you allow plenty of time, especially if you have more than one or two to make.

Corsages are perfect if the clothing has a decent structure to it, such as a shirt or a jacket. If your wearer's clothing is super-lightweight or fine, such as a silk dress, you might want to consider a ribbon-tie corsage or bouquet instead.

Pin-On Corsage

I often get asked to suggest an idea for the female members of the extended family, and a pin-on corsage - similar to the men's buttonhole - is the perfect little touch, finished with satin bows and pins.

ITEMS USED IN THIS DESIGN

These corsages are a pretty combination of natural tones – ivory, pinks and sage greens – with lots of fluffy pampas to create a lovely shape.

- **Base dried flowers** – Dried broom bloom and dried gypsophila.
- **Dried flowers and grasses** – Pampas grass, dried phalaris and lepidium.
- **Accessories** – Satin bows and pins.

The Method

1. Start in the same way as the buttonhole, with two or three little pieces of dried broom bloom. Cross them over each other at 45 degrees using the spiral technique (*see* page 30).
2. Add in some dried gypsophila and five stems of phalaris - three on one side and two on the other. I am trying to achieve a wider appearance than the buttonhole, which is straighter in shape.
3. Add in some fluffy pampas pieces at both sides for a fuller, more feminine look.
4. Add floral bind wire and cut the stems 3–4cm (1¼–1½in) past the wire.
5. Finish with a little ribbon bow to the front and two pins to attach the corsage on the back.

Broom bloom is a wonderful base flower to give structure. It is available in masses of different colours, from bleached white to the darkest dyed black, with pretty much every colour in-between.

Using flowers that naturally splay out is a good way to get a nice, open, almost triangular shape. This is perfect for corsages, which are often worn on a jacket lapel.

Using a few pieces of pampas, which have been broken off a longer stem and saved, is a great way to get a fluffy, feminine look for a corsage. This helps to create a perfect triangular shape.

You can cut your stems to any length, depending on how you plan to finish your corsage. The shorter the stems, the simpler the finishing will need to be. Allow enough room to tie your ribbon if you plan to use a bow.

If the fabric on your clothing is too light and flimsy to support a corsage and you don't want to create a hole in the delicate fabric, using a ribbon tie is a great alternative.

Ribbon-Tie Corsage

A ribbon-tie corsage around the wrist is a great alternative to a pin-on corsage. This beautiful design ties around the wrist with ribbon or hessian and can be easily taken off and reutilised as a bag charm or similar later in the day.

ITEMS USED IN THIS DESIGN

A beautiful palette of pastel tones create this pretty ribbon corsage, perfect for a summer wedding. You could use different coloured ribbons that match back to the wearer's outfit or go for something more rustic like a hessian ribbon.

- **Accessories** – Ribbon for the base and ties.
- **Foliage** – Preserved eucalyptus leaves.
- **Dried and preserved flowers** – Dried broom bloom, preserved gypsophila, dried statice, bunny tails and preserved hydrangea.

The Method

1. Cut a 14cm (5½in) length of ribbon, using the same colour as the ribbon you plan to use for the tie length. Fold both sides over and glue them down. This gives a nice clean edge to the ribbon piece that you will attach your flowers to before it is applied to the long ribbon length. The finished length of this piece will be approximately 8cm (3¼in).
2. Turn over the doubled ribbon piece and apply glue on the same side as the join. We will now apply your flowers over this piece so we want to hide the join.
3. Place your bigger leaves on both sides of the ribbon to hide it and provide a nice base to your design.
4. Next, add in layers and layers of your dried flowers, positioned to the edge, leaving a central section that can be covered later. Try to make a nice elongated rounded shape.
5. Choose a bigger flower, such as a piece of hydrangea, to cover the stems. Apply some glue and place the flower in the middle.
6. Once your arrangement is dry, add some glue to the reverse side and attach a long piece of ribbon that you can use to tie around the wrist. I would suggest a length of about 1 metre (1 yard).

Applying glue to your ribbon can be messy, so use a piece of paper beneath it to avoid glue staining your work surface. Have a cloth to hand to wipe away any glue from your fingers.

Don't make your corsage too wide as you want it to sit in the middle of the wrist, not splay out too much at either side. Wrists are small surface areas to cover, so don't get carried away with your design; smaller and rounder is better.

Think about other uses for your items as well as their intended purpose. For example, a corsage can be removed and tied to a bag, used as a dog collar or tied around a cake.

Using larger-headed flowers such as hydrangea means that you can make your corsage look more three-dimensional and hide a lot of the lower layer stems.

You can match your ribbons to the flowers or the wearer's dress. Choosing the right colour ribbon can really amplify a colour scheme so don't just opt for something obvious.

Creating your floral corsage on a separate piece of ribbon gives a clean, neat finish and gives it more stability.

Flower Girl Floral Hoop

Now I am going to show you how to create something a little different. This is a flower girl hoop, which you could adapt to a larger size for a bridesmaid too. It's a nice alternative to a bouquet or a posy and can be useful for a young flower girl. I will show you how to create this in a pastel-toned design but you could adapt this in any colour or floral style. The key is to have a ribbon tie at the centre to hide the stems and finish it nicely.

The Method

1. Start by creating two little posies in the same construction as a buttonhole (*see* page 73). These can be a little simpler than your buttonhole design because we are using two of them. I like to use cute little stems like bunny tails and phalaris.
2. Tie both posies on to the metal ring with floral bind wire, adding the second posy across the first so that the stems cross over each other. Secure them together with wire.
3. Cut the stems shorter as these will be hidden under your ribbon bow.
4. Wire a small piece of a larger flower over the middle of your posies to hide some of the stems.
5. Finally, add a ribbon bow across the flowers so it sits below your arrangements. This is the bottom of your design – the hoop can be carried at the top.

ITEMS USED IN THIS DESIGN

This is the perfect summer palette of pink, lilac, peach and sage green. All these colours have a lovely natural look, slightly washed out and very pretty. You could make this piece in any colour combination, so get creative with your ideas!

- **Accessories** – 15cm (6in)-wide gold metal hoop, and satin ribbon.
- **Dried flowers** – Dried broom bloom, dried phalaris, dried statice and bunny tails.
- **Preserved flower** – Preserved hydrangea.

Floral hoops are really easy to make and use only a handful of flowers. You could use any ring, such as white, gold or wooden, or a different metal shape such as a heart or triangle.

Use little broken stems that have been discarded to make smaller-scale items. This way you'll use as many of your flowers as possible with minimal waste.

Think about the scale of your flowers against the size of the hoop you have chosen. You could scale everything up and use a larger hoop with bigger bunches of flowers. Make sure you scale everything up or down accordingly.

If your hoop is going to be for a very young flower girl, choose stems that are not too delicate or that might easily be broken. You could also decorate with ribbons or bows to make your hoop more appealing to a young child.

You can add multiple layers of ribbons that hang down for a more bohemian look. Consider the ribbons you choose – using a variety of colours will make your hoop more fun, giving it a festival vibe, but keeping it simple will suit a more contemporary look.

Flower Crown

I absolutely love a flower crown! If you want to really stand out for your wedding or event, you can't go wrong with one. There is just something so special about going all out on your look with flowers through your hair. You can create a flower crown to match any theme or colour story – this one is made in a flower-heavy style but you could use a wildflower-foraged style or add foliage for a Grecian look.

Flower crowns are for anyone of any age – I absolutely encourage it! Little flower girls look so sweet wearing them, but give me a boho wedding complete with bridal flower crown any day. Just have fun with it!

The Method

1. Use lengths of floral wire to create your flower crown base. Starting with two pieces, I wind them together to make a sturdier piece of wire. I make two of these lengths and then cross them over at the middle to make the base extra sturdy and get the length that I want. Measure this on your head – make sure the length is long enough to mostly go around your head, leaving a little gap so that it can be tied looser or tighter when worn. Create a small loop with the wire at each end for the ribbon to attach through.
2. Add floral tape to the wire to give it a little more structure. You can tape the whole wire or just cover the sharp ends.
3. Separately create lots of little posies of dried and preserved flowers. I like to make these a little different to each other so that the look, once assembled, is more random and interesting, but you could do an all-one-variety version of this design (all hydrangea or all gypsophila, for example). Leave the bind wire a little longer than usual on these pieces as you will be attaching this to your wire headband.
4. Start at one side and face your first little posy outwards towards the end of the wire. Attach it with the bind wire that you have already applied to the posy and twist the ends of the wire to tightly secure it. Snip off any extra length of the bind wire.
5. Keep adding little posies until you get to the end, all in the same direction. The final posy can have some floral tape to cover the stems.
6. Cut two long lengths of ribbon – at least 45cm (18in) (but make them as long or short as you want, depending on whether you want a large bow or something simpler). Tie them on to the little loops at either side. Cut each end of the ribbon in a nice 45-degree angle to avoid fraying.

ITEMS USED IN THIS DESIGN

This is a hot summer colour palette – all the shades of red and pink come together to make a gorgeous combination in this design. I love the two-tone look here, but you can create this in absolutely any colour combination or use only one colour.

- **Accessories** – White floral wire, white floral tape and satin ribbon.
- **Dried flowers** – Dried broom bloom, preserved gypsophila, dried achillea, dried statice, bunny tails and dried phalaris.
- **Preserved flower** – Preserved hydrangea.

OPPOSITE: Flower crowns can be a fun way to add a splash of colour to your wedding or event. You can create them in any combination of colours and styles, but smaller-headed flowers that are lighter tend to work better.

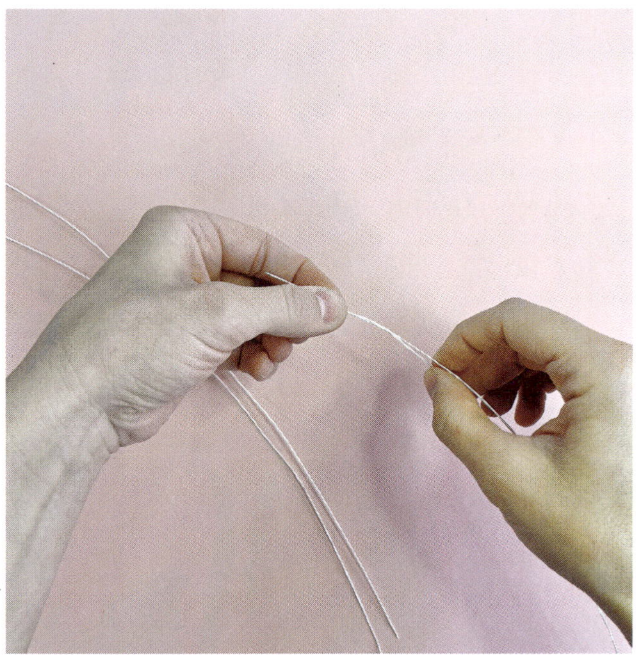

Think about the colours of the wearer's hair and the flowers when you are selecting the colour of the floral wire. Darker greens will blend in better with darker hair and white might work better for blonde or grey hair.

Wrapping the wire with floral tape isn't completely necessary. It gives more stability and can help to hide the sharp ends but it takes a long time, so decide if you think it is necessary.

I like to use a variety of stems for my flower crowns. I mix these up for each little posy so that the finished look is much more irregular. You can also use up broken pieces of stems that would otherwise have been thrown away.

Smaller-scale flowers tend to work better for flower crowns. Just remember, the bigger the posies you make, the larger the flower crown will look once it is worn.

Flower crowns offer a way to maximise your wedding or event, adding drama for a bride or birthday girl. They look really sweet on little girls too and avoid the need to hold on to something.

Think about the finishing you want. Ribbons can be in a contrast colour, you could use different sizes or combine materials such as satin, grosgrain or organza.

Hair combs are a lovely way to add some floral interest to your hair and can be worn in a variety of different ways. You can attach above a veil, wear alone or wear with your hair swept to the side.

Hair Comb

The final project in this chapter is a lovely little finishing touch, perfect for a bride or bridesmaid. This floral hair comb can be attached to the hair just above the veil, or can replace the need for a veil completely. I tend to use flowers or foliage that match back to the rest of the flowers, but I have created hair combs for specific guests to match their outfits too. The hair comb I'm about to show you is a lovely autumnal design featuring flowers, foliage and touches of pampas grass.

The Method

1. Just like we did for the Ribbon-Tie Corsage (*see* page 84), we are going to create a folded piece of ribbon to use for our base. Secure it with glue and then add glue to one side to start applying your stems. Start with large pieces of foliage, trying to imagine how they will look in your hair. Don't make it too long as you want it to sit centrally and not show at either side of your head from the front.
2. Add a touch of pampas and some little pieces of dried broom bloom for colour. Feed each stem under the foliage stems to secure. If you need to add a little more glue, you can.
3. Once you have added all the flowers and foliage you want, add some glue to the middle of your design. Press something large into this to hide the stems – here I'm using a perfect piece of foliage and two pieces of hydrangea that I taped together.
4. Once your floral piece is dry you can turn it over, glue along the length of ribbon and attach it to the plastic hair comb. I use little clips to hold it in place while it dries.
5. Once it is dry, glue one more piece of ribbon – cut neatly to the exact length of the comb – over the back of the comb to tidy up all the mechanics.

ITEMS USED IN THIS DESIGN

This is a stunning autumnal colour palette of rusts, orange, browns, greens and natural tones. Adding in touches of bunny tails and natural pampas grass softens the whole look.

- **Accessories** – Clear plastic hair comb and satin ribbon.
- **Dried flowers and grasses** – Dried broom bloom, dried wheat, bunny tails and pampas grass.
- **Preserved foliage** – Preserved green eucalyptus populus, preserved green eucalyptus and preserved brown eucalyptus.
- **Preserved flower** – Preserved hydrangea.

I make floral hair combs on a base of ribbon using the same method as the Ribbon-Tie Corsage, but you could use a hessian base for a more rustic look.

Covering the centre and all the lower stems is a perfect way to clean up your design. You could use a few pieces of hydrangea or some smaller-scale roses for this. Alternatively, fluffy pampas will add a good covering.

Don't make your hair comb arrangement too long as you don't want to see the flowers from the front when it is worn. Hold a few stems in place and see what it looks like before you glue it down. Shaping the flowers slightly downwards looks best as the head and comb are rounded.

Find little items to help you – here I found some little clips to hold the ribbon and glue in place. You could also use safety pins or paper clips.

Using a little piece of ribbon cleans up the finished look. Always think about how your item will be finished to make it look as good as possible. You could use some hessian, patterned or shiny paper, or fabric here too.

MIRLAH RICHARDSON, WEDDING PHOTOGRAPHER

Mirlah has been a full-time wedding photographer for the last three years. Before that, she worked in the wedding industry for over ten years as a wedding co-ordinator and events manager. Her work has been featured in leading industry websites including Rock My Wedding, Love My Dress and Whimsical Wonderland Weddings. She has also been named one of the top 50 wedding photographers for 2024 and 2025 by *Professional Photo* magazine.

Tell us a little about yourself and your photography style.

Hi, I'm Mirlah, the heart behind Mirl & Co. I'm a wedding photographer based in Derbyshire, passionate about capturing love stories in the most authentic and joyful way. My style embraces natural light, vibrant colours and genuine moments. I'm all about creating images that feel timeless yet relaxed, full of warmth, personality and a touch of the unexpected. I absolutely love working with couples who throw the rule book out the window and are unapologetically themselves, making every wedding a unique story to tell.

What trends have you noticed in wedding and event floristry over the years?

I'm all about the 'you do you' approach. Trends come and go, but if you choose what you love and what truly represents you, that'll always be the best kind of trend. Lately, I've been loving how couples are embracing wild textures and bold colour palettes. Reds and pinks aren't just reserved for the sweet and romantic any more; they're giving off bold, retro, disco energy – and I'm here for it. It's all about having fun with your wedding style!

Sustainability is also having a major moment, with florists using locally sourced, seasonal blooms and ditching foam for eco-friendly designs. And, of course, dried flowers are making a strong comeback. Not only do they bring that cool, textural charm, but couples get to keep them as beautiful keepsakes long after the party's over.

Tell us a little about how you capture flowers in different kinds of venues and which specific items are the most impactful to photograph.

Flowers are such an integral part of the visual story. In bright, airy venues, I love using natural light to highlight their vibrant colours and delicate details. In darker spaces, I play with contrast to make the florals pop against moodier backdrops. While large installations like floral arches or suspended designs make a bold impact, I believe even the smallest details, like a beautifully crafted bouquet or delicate bud vases, can be incredibly striking when framed thoughtfully.

Can you recommend the best places in a venue to capture your photos?

When looking for the best spots in a venue to capture photos, I'm always on the lookout for beautiful natural light. As a documentary photographer, my goal is to tell the story wherever it unfolds, but if I have control over the location, I gravitate towards spaces with plenty of natural light, like large windows that flood the room with softness and warmth.

I also love incorporating architectural details that add depth and context to the images. Textured walls, unique flooring or interesting furniture can all help anchor a photo in the character of the venue. After all, couples choose their venue for a reason, so it's important to showcase those meaningful details.

I'm especially drawn to pockets of light where dramatic contrasts come to life – moody shadows meeting streams of harsh sunlight. There's something magical about how colours, especially florals, pop in these conditions, adding vibrancy and emotion to the story I'm capturing.

How does lighting and natural light affect the way flowers appear in photos?

Lighting is everything! Natural light brings out the true-to-life colours and textures of florals, making them appear fresh and vibrant. When working outside, soft, diffused light, like on an overcast day or in shaded areas, helps avoid harsh shadows and blown-out highlights, especially with neutral and white colour palettes. The magic of golden hour adds warmth and a dreamy glow, while harsh midday sun can sometimes wash out colours or create strong contrasts. However, with the right techniques, even midday sun can be used creatively.

Even after dark, there's room for creative lighting. Analogue and flash photography are making a big comeback, and I love embracing those nostalgic retro vibes. Using direct flash in the evening can create a fun, party atmosphere that couples really enjoy, adding variety and excitement to their final gallery.

Can you share a memorable moment where flowers played a large role in one of your previous weddings?
I always get so excited to see the flowers on a wedding day. It's such a beautiful moment when the vision truly comes to life in a burst of colour and joy. One wedding that stands out was an autumn celebration with two brides, where one wore a dark floral silk gown. She looked like a floral goddess, and the gown perfectly matched the stunning bouquet she carried – it was a match made in flower heaven.

What is your best collaboration suggestion between yourself and the florist?
Lately, I've fallen in love with the rise of the micro wedding – those intimate celebrations surrounded by your closest people. It's a smaller gathering, but the room is filled with so much love. I feel so lucky to capture these beautiful love stories, and what I love most is how a smaller wedding doesn't mean sacrificing the special details that make the day uniquely yours.

Sarah and I had the privilege of working on a stunning micro wedding together. With just five guests in attendance, the day was as intimate as it was beautiful. While the couple were the obvious stars of the show, the bride's gorgeous oversized dried flower bouquet was a showstopper. The rich autumnal colours perfectly matched the bride's thrifted orange shoes, adding a thoughtful, personal touch to the day. It just goes to show that even in an intimate setting, the details can truly make a celebration unforgettable.

Have you noticed any common mistakes with floral design from a photographic point of view?
This isn't something that happens that often, I don't want to offend anyone.

When it comes to photographing show-stopping floral arrangements, the backdrop plays a crucial role. For example, a light, bright white wall paired with flowers in similar tones can make them fade into the background. Add in a stream of sunlight and (often) a white dress, and the result can be washed out. It's important to consider where the light is coming from – does the space get any natural light at all? By thinking about the bigger picture, you can choose colours and textures that don't compete with the florals.

Mirlah Richardson. (Photo: Laura Adams).

Finally, do you have any tips for florists to help ensure their work looks amazing in photos?
I absolutely love when flowers and arrangements can be moved, reused and repurposed throughout the day. A ceremony backdrop that later becomes the showstopper at the top table, table decorations that find new life by adorning the evening reception areas, and bud vases that can be placed around the venue, by signage or next to the cake, every piece has a chance to shine again. Even bouquets can have a dedicated spot, not just left behind on a chair but displayed beautifully until they're needed. Flowers are such a beautiful element that truly elevate a photo, and I love making sure they're always visible, adding that extra touch to every moment captured.

Using a thoughtful combination of flower arrangements can simply bring an area to life. Here I added one large arrangement on one side of a sign and popped two little bud vases on the other side.

Room and Event Flowers

So far, we have covered all the ideas you will need for the flowers for your wedding party and guests. Now I want to show you how to take your wedding decor up to the next level with lots of ideas on how to dress your event space. You can use these designs for any event; I will help you create pieces that you can use to dress any table or room. These items will also work beautifully for your home too – you can either create them specifically for your home or reuse them in your home after your event.

When it comes to decorating a space, more is definitely more! The more items you have the time to create, the more special the effect will be. Bear in mind that it is much easier and quicker to make multiples of one design than lots of different items that you need to retrain yourself for each time. You can get into quite a good routine making the same item over and over again, so you can get through the work much more quickly.

This chapter will walk you through the main ideas for creations that will sit on tables or the floor; the simplest idea being little bud vase arrangements (*see* page 100), moving through to more complicated items such as floor-standing meadow arrangements (*see* page 114).

WHAT DO YOU NEED FOR AN EVENT SPACE?

Before you start designing your event flowers, think about the journey you will go on during the day at your event. First, consider your arrival and how you would like to dress that space, creating a welcoming area for your guests to get a sneak peek into the theme of your event.

Once you have that space sorted, think about the next stages of your day and what floral items you will need to bring the rest of your space to life. If you are creating for a wedding, do you want to dress the aisle or the end of the aisle? Will you reuse those designs for your wedding breakfast tables? If you are planning a meal or party, do you have tables you want to dress or are you planning on creating a feature wall for a photobooth or a speaker's podium? Once you have thought through the day and which parts you want to create your flowers for, you will be able to think about how many and which kinds of arrangements will work best.

Using table centrepieces on plinths can make them look wonderful, especially if they are paired with draping fabric and candles. Not all your arrangements need to be large scale; you can make smaller ones really special with a few styling additions.

Bud Vase Trio

I love a little trio of bud vases. Such a simple design and quick to create, these little gems are the perfect touch of florals for your tables. They work for any table configuration – round tables look lovely with three to five vases in the middle, while long banquet tables look great with bud vases placed sporadically along their length. I love to design things in groups of three because things just look more harmonious in odd-numbered groupings. Therefore, I design my bud vases in three different designs so the final look – no matter how many you make – is eclectic and mismatched.

I will show you how to create three different designs in the same style and colour palette; the first two are simpler, using fewer stems, while the third is a little more special.

STEMS USED IN THIS DESIGN

This palette is soft and muted with a lovely range of pastel tones. Each bud vase has a slightly different colour story so that each looks a little different. One has touches of sage, another is mostly blues and ivory, and the final one is slightly more special and contains all the colours of the palette.

- **Base dried flowers** – Dried broom bloom and preserved gypsophila.
- **Large focal flower** – Preserved hydrangea.
- **Foliage** – Blue-green eucalyptus cinerea.
- **Dried flowers and grasses** – Dried lavender, dried statice, dried phalaris, dried wheat, bunny tails and pampas grass.

Bud vases look nice placed in groups of three; you can keep one or two of the buds in a really simple design and make one more special. This will give a special look overall but will be much simpler to create.

Bud vases are the simplest way to create some interest for tables, welcome areas and much more. They can be made with literally any combination of flowers in any colours. They are unsung little heroes!

Vase 1: Touches of Sage

The Method

1. Begin your design by taking one stem of the filler flower dried broom bloom, crossed over the back in a 45-degree angle, and one stem of preserved gypsophila for a bit of height.
2. Next add in three stems of phalaris at different heights (one or two of these can be quite high to create some drama) and a stem of dried wheat.
3. Cut your stems to fit your bud vase and allow them to splay out a little.

Consider the shape of your bud vase carefully as it will affect the size of the arrangement you create. Smaller openings on vases require fewer flowers to fill them, while rounded vases need some shorter lengths to secure the flowers in place, even if the opening is small.

Using flowers in little groups of three looks really attractive. Keep the stems all at different heights; some can be left really long to create drama.

Vase 2: Blues and Ivories

The Method

1. For this little bud vase design, which is also very simple, start with two stems of dried broom bloom and one stem of dried statice. Cross these stems at a 45-degree angle.
2. Next, add in three stems of bunny tails, again making one or two of these stems taller than the rest. Add a little pampas grass on the other side and five or six stems of lavender towards the back.
3. Cut your stems and place into your bud vase.

Using bold contrasting colours adds more interest to your bud vases. I only use a few stems in each design so each one needs to add a lot of value.

Adding little pieces of pampas grass fills the neck of the vase, helping other stems stay in place.

Vase 3: Pastel Palette

The Method

1. Start with two stems of broom bloom, two stems of phalaris (placed at varying heights) and one stem of dried wheat at the other side.
2. Now for the most focal blooms – add one stem of foliage at one side and a small head of preserved hydrangea at the front.
3. Cut your stems, making sure that the hydrangea is short enough to sit on the top of the vase at the very bottom of the design.

Using a few stems of grasses that have lots of movement fluffs out your arrangements at the sides, making them look more interesting. Use lots of dried grasses in your bud vase designs for a compelling look.

One large piece of hydrangea will fill the opening of your vase well, so make sure that you cut this stem to sit right above the neck of the vase.

OPPOSITE: Simple styling works really well for bud vases. Place the vases in little groups for a simple but effective look. Ensure your fabric drapes in a nice pool on the floor for a really rich effect.

Table and Floor-Standing Arrangements

Table centrepieces are wonderful arrangements that make the middle of a table look beautiful. They are circular designs to be enjoyed from all angles and they can be made with any combination of different flowers, ranging from wildflower arrangements to flower-heavy designs.

Compote Arrangement

Perhaps my favourite room decor arrangement – the compote design. I love this little pot of goodness! You can use any little open bowl to create something like this; just bear in mind that the larger the bowl, the bigger the arrangement. These little pedestal bowls are quite small at 10cm (4in) across, but they create a finished arrangement that is approximately 30cm (12in) across. As you design all the way around – turning the bowl as you create to make sure that all sides look lovely – this could be used in the middle of a round table and enjoyed from all angles.

STEMS USED IN THIS DESIGN

I am obsessed with this colour story! I will always love red and pink together, but a little pop of yellow adds an unexpected moment that makes this colour palette really sing. I have toned it down a little with the use of some fluffy darker-brown-toned ferns, so the deep colour is still light and airy.

- **Base materials** – Eco floral foam and preserved moss.
- **Large focal flowers** – Preserved hydrangea and preserved roses.
- **Dried flowers and foliage** – Dried ferns, dried achillea, bunny tails and preserved gypsophila.

The Method

1. To create a compote arrangement, begin with your eco floral foam (*see* page 14 for a little about floral foam and its impact on the environment). Cut the foam with scissors so that it is slightly bigger than the bowl, can be pushed in and will sit tightly. It's OK if it sits a little higher than the bowl; this will give you more room to work as you design and the foam will still be covered by your flowers. Cover the top roughly with some preserved moss so that you can't see the foam clearly. You can push a few stems of broom bloom through the moss to keep it in place if you need to, but the flowers you will be adding will also do that for you.
2. Since this design is created mostly with preserved large-headed blooms, I want to go straight to work adding some of the larger flowers to cover the base. Use four stems of hydrangea that you have previously split from larger heads (*see* page 33 for how to split and retape your stems). Place these all around at different heights, allowing some to fall below the edge of the foam and cover the bowl a little.
3. Add five or six preserved roses. I have reflexed the petals (*see* page 36) to open up these roses and give more drama, as well as making them bigger to help cover the foam. Place these all around at different heights, filling in any holes you have. After adding these, your bowl should be mostly covered with flowers at all sides of the design.
4. Next, add some fluffier longer stems. Here I am using dried ferns, which are fluffy and light but have strong stems so will sit tall in your design. Add these asymmetrically – one high on one side and one low on the other. Add some gypsophila low down at another side of the design and anywhere else you think could use a little splash of texture.
5. Finally, add your pop flowers – I have used three stems of achillea (keeping two of the stems long for drama), as well as three or four stems of matching bunny tails, all placed at different heights.

Table compote designs are a real show stopper and are quite easy to make. They can be used for any number of different things such as centrepieces, welcome signs, cake tables and registrar's tables.

You can use any type of bowl that you like for this arrangement. Bear in mind that your finished arrangement will be about three times larger than its bowl, so use a bowl size that is much smaller than you want the finished arrangement to be.

Use big-headed flowers for this style of arrangement to fill in the space really quickly. You can then add taller pieces here and there for interest.

Turn your arrangement around as you make it to ensure that all sides look beautiful – you can use a lazy Susan to easily move it around. This is a 360-degree design that should be enjoyed from all angles.

Ferns add fluffy romance vibes to your arrangement. They come fresh and you can dry them yourself, but beware, they do shed and make a lot of mess.

Really think about your colour palette when you are designing. Adding a splash of bright colour to an arrangement really makes all the other colours pop.

Table-Standing Arrangement

An alternative idea for a table centrepiece is to create your design with floral foam only and have it sit flat on the table. This is useful if you want to make different-sized designs and not to be stuck following the dimensions of your pedestal bowls. These arrangements also work really well placed down your wedding aisle, on registrar's tables or cake tables. Basically, this is probably your most versatile event floral item.

I'm going to show you a small-scale arrangement that would work well for a table centrepiece, but you could also scale this design for more dramatic installations – perhaps at the end of an aisle or next to a welcome sign. The design I'm going to make is attractive from all sides but has a focus to the front. If you want to make this work for the middle of the table, turn it around as you make it to ensure all sides look beautiful.

The Method

1. Begin your design with a block of floral foam. You can cut this down with scissors to the size you need. For this design I have cut one brick in half.
2. Next, I add foliage at different heights. I add this all the way around the block approximately as I imagine the finished look taking shape. I place one stem higher at the back than the rest and a palm leaf on three different sides. Once this stage is done, my design is really taking shape and I just fill it in with the rest of my flowers.
3. Add small stems of broom bloom all around at different heights; I'm using two different colours for more interest. You can easily break off smaller stems of this flower but you might find you still need to cut the ends with secateurs so that they slide easily into the foam. I cut at a 45-degree angle as this makes the stems much easier to move into the foam. You don't want to have to rearrange your stems too many times as the foam loses its shape and eventually breaks apart, but if you place a stem and it looks or feels wrong, you can remove it and replace it in a better position.
4. Add small pieces of eucalyptus parvifolia foliage throughout.
5. Now to add your preserved blooms. These will fill out your design and cover over the foam. Start with the hydrangea, which you can cut fairly short so that it provides a good base covering. Preserved hydrangea stems are quite malleable and they bend easily so you will need to tape smaller pieces onto leftover hard stems (I save harder stems once I've cut them for this purpose). Add three roses at different heights, facing towards the front slightly.
6. Finally, plug any holes with short pieces of pampas grass and add a few longer stems for added drama. Check the back of your design and fill any holes with pampas and broom bloom.

ITEMS USED IN THIS DESIGN

This is a gothic-style colour palette with lots of black and contrasting tones. The burgundy and sand-coloured roses add different levels of colour, making this a perfect winter colour palette. You could add extra pink to soften the look or touches of rust for an autumnal vibe.

- **Base material** – Floral foam.
- **Base dried flowers** – Dried broom bloom.
- **Large focal flowers** – Preserved hydrangea and preserved roses.
- **Dried foliage** – Dried palm leaves.
- **Preserved foliage** – Brown beech leaves, eucalyptus parvifolia and baby blue eucalyptus.
- **Dried grasses** – Black and natural pampas grass.

Floor-standing arrangements are made using floral foam, which allows them to sit flat on the table or surface you want to place them on. This arrangement can be scaled up or down to suit your needs.

Floral foam is quite delicate and can only be used once or twice before it starts to collapse, so don't remove and replace your stems too many times.

I have used beech leaves for this design as they create a lovely shape, but you can get all kinds of preserved foliage for this use. Foliage is available in lots of natural tones, but beware, sometimes the dye and sap can leak out and stain clothing.

Getting the shape right first with your base flowers and foliage makes creating your design much easier. Use the first layer to create your shape and then fill in with your choice of flowers.

Using a few different varieties of foliage adds more interest to your creations for a wilder and more natural look.

Angle your most impactful flowers slightly towards the front for them to be appreciated more easily if your arrangement will be viewed from one side. If it is to be viewed from all angles, make sure you use flowers all around.

I always add pampas grass last as it is the perfect stem to add drama. It also fills in any little holes, so you can hide the floral foam.

For arrangements with lots of deep dark tones, consider adding a few softer neutral tones to balance the whole look. Adding plenty of foliage also helps to give a more natural look.

Floor-Standing Meadow Arrangement

This larger-scale display is similar to the Table-standing Arrangement (*see* page 110) but is more dramatic, with longer stems that make it look as though it is growing out of the ground naturally. This is a lovely focal arrangement that would work well either at the beginning or the end of the aisle and allows you to create some serious wow factor. You could use it for an event doorway or place two together at the foot of a dining table. I make this using a little wooden tray that the floral foam is placed into, so it will last for a long time after your event.

The Method

1. I like to create taller arrangements on a little base of some kind to support the floral foam. Cut pieces of foam to fit the tray – a little bigger than the opening so that you have to force them in – keeping them firmly in place. You could also glue pieces of foam onto a piece of sturdy cardboard as a more cost-effective alternative.
2. Cover your foam with preserved moss and secure it in place with some shorter stems of broom bloom. This design is fairly open and you can see through the stems to the base, so we want the base to be more attractive than the floral foam.
3. Next, place your longest foliage stems at the back. I'm using beech leaves, which splay out nice and wide for a more even coverage at the back of the design.
4. Add a nice covering on the front of the base with your hydrangea – I've used three shades here to break up the colours nicely. I place these at varying heights but mostly along the bottom, with one or two longer stems mixed in randomly. Also add a few of the very long focal flowers – achillea works well as its stems are so strong they can be kept really long. Add two or three preserved roses.
5. Next, add lots of fluffy, open and gauzy textural flowers – here I have used dried ferns and preserved gypsophila. Fill in any holes with more roses, slightly angle them forwards so you can appreciate them in all their glory.
6. Add a few stems of pampas grass at the back and in any holes at the sides and front. Pampas grass is puffy so it plugs any gaps you might have perfectly.
7. Finally, add some pops of colour at different heights. Here I used three stems of yellow ochre achillea and five stems of yellow bunny tails, both with fairly sturdy stems so they can achieve that wonderful height.

ITEMS USED IN THIS DESIGN

This is a very bold and dramatic colour palette, which is a twist on an autumnal colour story. We used a range of classic autumnal shades from brown to rust and red, but added ochre yellow as an unexpected pop. Little dashes of pink soften the look.

- **Base materials** – Floral foam, a wooden tray and preserved moss.
- **Dried flowers** – Dried broom bloom, bunny tails and preserved gypsophila.
- **Large focal flowers** – Preserved hydrangea, preserved roses and dried achillea.
- **Foliage –** Preserved brown beech leaves, dried ferns and pampas grass.

OPPOSITE: Floor-standing arrangements are going to bring you lots of drama wherever you place them! You can arrange them in groups for maximum appeal or use one or two in special places. Use stems that create height at the back of the arrangement for the most drama.

Floor-standing meadow arrangements can have the flowers placed more sparsely, so I use moss to cover the floral foam. Moss comes in many different colours, so you can have it match the flowers or use a natural colour.

Foliage comes in nice strong lengths that can be used to create drama at the back of a floor-standing arrangement. Remove any broken or ripped leaves before you begin.

Use some larger-headed flowers at the base to cover some of the moss. Hydrangeas are great for this as they can be broken into smaller pieces where needed.

As this is a meadow arrangement, I use light and open flowers such as gypsophila as the stems are long and the flowers are open and wispy. You can also use ferns for this.

Adding in some touches of fluffy pampas help to cover the base of the arrangement and bring a little softness to your design.

Little pops of bright colour can really transform a colour palette, making your arrangement go from something standard to something really eye-catching. Use these pops of colour sparingly for the most impact.

Meadow arrangements are versatile and can be used in many different areas of your event, so make sure you feature them in as many places as possible throughout your day. Add a disco ball or two to take your display to the next level.

Registrar's Table Arrangement

The final room decor design is a really versatile arrangement that can be used on a registrar's table at the end of the aisle and then moved to the top table for your wedding breakfast. You could also use a series of these along the length of a banquet table. If you are creating flowers for an event, this is a perfect focal point that has a lot of drama and can be placed on any presentation table. This long arrangement is made with floral foam, but could alternatively be made by creating three floor-standing table arrangements and pushing them together, allowing you to use them in different ways during your event.

The Method

1. This is quite a large design so I use a whole floral foam block to create the base. If your flowers are fairly open and you want more of a sparse look, you can cover your foam with preserved moss. However, as this is a fairly dense design with lots of stems and some pampas, which fills in the holes really well, I don't need to use moss.
2. Add the preserved eucalyptus cinerea. Its branches are long and sturdy so we can quickly get the overall shape we are looking for. Make sure you get lots of width here to make this arrangement a good length. Add this foliage throughout to create a lovely shape, focusing the length at the sides.
3. Add in lots of complementary lengths of gypsophila. I used dried gypsophila here as the stems have much more stability and I'm trying to get width to my design. Use shorter stems of broom bloom here too to fill in space.
4. Fill in a lot of the shape with dried grasses and flowers. I add lots of lepidium and more broom bloom as well as some longer, more focal pieces of ruscus. Place the ruscus asymmetrically to make a more interesting design. Play with heights here too to ensure your final design looks relaxed.
5. Add your focal blooms. Here I used seven preserved roses in three different shades; try to angle them forwards a little to make the most of each flower. I also reflexed the petals to open up the bloom and make a more dramatic appearance (*see* page 36).
6. Finally, add some romance with your pampas grasses and a scattering of bunny tails at different heights and in groups of three. I add some eucalyptus nicholii now at different heights – it adds a lovely movement to the design. Plug any holes with little stems of pampas, especially at the back. You can also cut short lengths of large-leaved eucalyptus stems and put these around the back to fill in any space.

ITEMS USED IN THIS DESIGN

This arrangement is a classic but beautiful design with lots of gorgeous roses in three different shades: ivory, sand and peach. I use pretty gypsophila, shots of ruscus, and fluffy pampas and bunny tails to soften it. The idea was to have a lovely mix of pretty flowers with lots of different foliage for a romantic look.

- **Base material** – Floral foam.
- **Base dried flowers** – Dried broom bloom and dried gypsophila.
- **Large focal flowers** – Preserved roses in three different shades.
- **Preserved eucalyptus** – Preserved eucalyptus nicholii and preserved eucalyptus cinerea.
- **Dried foliage and grasses** – Dried ruscus, dried lepidium, bunny tails and pampas grass.

OPPOSITE: A little bit of styling can take your registrar's arrangement up to the next level. Add some simple fabric draping underneath and a few candles or bud vases to complete your look.

HENRY BAMFORD & SONS

The larger the floral foam block you use, the bigger your arrangement will be. To get the length, use one whole block, but you could cut the block up to make it smaller.

Use long lengths of foliage to create the shape and get the desired width. You can break off smaller pieces to use in the middle of your design but you will need to cut the ends sharply with your clippers to poke them into the foam.

For light and romantic-style designs, I use a lot of gypsophila to get an open and pretty look. Using a couple of different shades adds more interest.

Ruscus is a lovely strong stem that can be used to create long designs. It comes in many colours, including gold and silver for something extra special at Christmas time. You can also easily spray paint ruscus to your desired colour.

Using a few shades of roses together gives a more natural look and adds dimension to your creations. Since roses come in a number of natural tones, it's a nice idea to emulate nature and use a few shades at a time.

When you think your design is finished, do one last check and see if you can squeeze in a little more pampas or foliage, and take your work to the next level.

Registrar's table arrangements are so pretty and make a lovely focal design for the end of your aisle. Make sure your design is not too tall as you will sit at this table to sign your documents and you want to be able to see over the arrangement.

Flower clouds make a strong statement for the end of your aisle. Using multiple clouds can be a great way of filling a large warehouse-style space. Hang them at varying heights for a more interesting look.

Epic Installations

Now let's take your floral knowledge up to the next level! The next few pages will show you how to create more challenging pieces for your wedding or event. These pieces are large and more complex to make, so make sure to allow plenty of time. You might need to have a couple of attempts, or simply allow time to redo some parts until you feel your pieces are perfect, but rest assured, once you can master arrangements on this scale, your event is going to be a true showstopper!

WHY CONSIDER LARGE INSTALLATIONS FOR YOUR EVENT?

There are a number of reasons why you might want to consider creating florals on a large scale. First and foremost, you are going to get that drama that will make your event even more memorable. Large instals tend to capture a lot of attention from your guests and also create more impactful and dramatic photography; most photographers will be excited to see a large arrangement at your venue as they too know their work is now going to be next level. Having a focal arrangement at the end of your aisle, for example, would provide the perfect backdrop for your ceremony and give you an ideal place to take portrait photos. You could set up your flowers to create a lovely spot for guest photos or for a photo booth.

You might have a venue that has high ceilings, is a wide open space or has a staircase that would benefit from a large installation piece. Using one big arrangement can sometimes add more drama than lots of little pieces, and it focuses your budget too.

Finally, you might have one particular area that you would like to pay special attention to such as an aisle, sweetheart table, long table or backdrop. An epic installation would perfectly highlight one part of your venue, therefore elevating the whole event.

Hanging additional items from your flower clouds is a great way of making them more interesting. Use disco balls or hanging foliage, drapery or LED tea lights.

Hanging Flower Cloud

There's nothing quite like a hanging flower cloud, sometimes called a flower bomb – the ultimate floral piece that just oozes wow factor. Once you master this design, you can change up some of the detail to work better for your venue. I am going to show you how to create a long oblong-shaped arrangement, but you could make this as a ball shape or create multiple clouds that hang together as a group. This cloud is made with dried flowers and lots of foliage but you can make this design in any of my signature styles. It works particularly well with lots of pampas grasses as they 'fill in' the design beautifully and cover all the mechanics perfectly.

The Method

1. For hanging cloud-style arrangements, start by creating a strong base. I use eco floral foam wrapped with chicken wire in a long oblong shape. I wanted a really large arrangement here, so I used four blocks of floral foam. The chicken wire can be cut to size with pliers – wear gloves to protect your hands because the wire is very sharp once cut. You can bunch up the chicken wire with your hands to secure it.
2. I make little loops on the top and at either side of the chicken wire to create little handles to hang from. Run some lengths of floral bind wire through the loops and hang from a frame (I use a clothes rack from IKEA for this purpose); alternatively, hang from a feature on your ceiling such as a beam. You can remove the bind wire when you hang your cloud in the venue and use fishing wire instead – this disappears from view once you stand back, yet it is very strong.
3. Begin to add your base layer to create your initial shape – I use long stems of eucalyptus cinerea. Create a 360 design (meaning it can be enjoyed from the back and sides as well as the front).
4. Add different types of foliage to begin filling out your design. I used a couple of colours to create interest.
5. Next I add a whole bunch of dried broom bloom in a lovely rich red colour. I break off bits, snip the ends at an angle with my secateurs so the stems go into the foam really easily, and add throughout my hanging design.
6. At this stage, I can start to see where we will have holes that show the mechanics (the foam and the chicken wire) so I push handfuls of preserved moss into the chicken wire and between the foliage stems. Secure it with little stems of broom bloom if you need to.
7. Add in your focal flowers now in prominent places. While this is a 360 design, you should still focus your main larger-headed flowers to the front where they will be more appreciated.
8. Add in stems of dried flowers and grasses now at different lengths. Position all your stems splaying slightly outwards all around from the centre.
9. Add your hanging amaranthus underneath – I added it all the way along the base at different lengths. You will need to tape your amaranthus stems onto stronger discarded stems that will push into the foam more easily, as amaranthus stems are very soft when preserved (use the technique described on page 15).
10. Add in more and more foliage. You can cut the foliage into short pieces that can be added to cover the chicken wire. Don't forget the back, sides and underneath of your design so that the arrangement looks good from all angles.

ITEMS USED IN THIS DESIGN

For this foliage-heavy design I use lots of different foliage in a lovely range of natural green tones, as well as bright-green hanging amaranthus, which helps to create the drama I am looking for. The palette also includes lots of autumnal accents: reds, rusts, yellows and a range of orange tones.

- **Base materials** – Eco floral foam, chicken wire, floral bind wire and preserved moss.
- **Base dried flower** – Dried broom bloom.
- **Various foliage types** – Eucalyptus cinerea in green and brown, eucalyptus nicholii, eucalyptus parvifolia and hanging amaranthus.
- **Dried flowers and grasses** – Wheat and helichrysum.
- **Large focal flowers** – Palm cups, protea and achillea.

Think about the space in which you are hanging your flower or foliage cloud – once *in situ*, it will look much smaller if the space is vast. Consider the size and shape before you begin and make your cloud size work accordingly.

The longer you make your caged floral foam block construction at the beginning, the larger your finished arrangement will be. If you are making a sparse design that will show the base, you can trap moss inside the construction before you start adding your flowers.

Begin with strong structured stems to help you get your shape quickly. Strong foliage stems work well for this or you could also use ruscus or pampas.

Using a mixture of foliage colours can help your design look more dimensional. Preserved foliage colours range from greens all the way through to dark burgundies and reds – there are even painted varieties available.

Focus your colourful dried flowers towards the front of the arrangement but ensure there is some interest at the back of the cloud too as it will also be viewed from the back. Add your dried flowers at varying heights for more interest.

Create your flower cloud before your event. You may lose a few stems when transporting it to your venue, but it will be much quicker to create it at a height that is manageable for you and then raise it into position.

Arch Arrangement

Arch arrangements are a wonderful way of creating a simpler design that still has a lot of impact. Some venues have an arch that you can use; alternatively, you can buy metal arches online in a round or square shape. Square arches allow you to add draping fabric, which is much trickier to do on a round arch. You can also create more than one arrangement for your arch. If I create more than one, I prefer that they are different sizes and I place them at varying heights - for example, one on the top right and another on the lower left.

The Method

1. I begin by creating this piece on a frame in my studio. It's much easier to create this arrangement at standing height and then transfer to the arch, so I use an affordable clothes rail for this purpose. Attach your floral foam block to the stand using two long pieces of floral bind wire. Make sure the pieces are long enough so you can use them to attach your arrangement to your arch; you don't want to have to replace them for longer lengths once this arrangement is finished.
2. Add in long stems of eucalyptus cinerea to begin creating your shape. I use longer lengths on the ends and smaller pieces in the middle.
3. Break off pieces of dried broom bloom and snip the ends at an angle before adding them throughout the arrangement.
4. Next add your focal flowers towards the centre of the design. All stems should be added splaying outwards from the centre in each direction. I add these all at different heights to add more dimension to the overall look. It's a good idea to have the flowers focused on the lower side of the arrangement as the top side won't be seen once it is placed high up on an arch.
5. Add the smaller dried flower stems throughout, leaving some long stems at the edges to make your arrangement as big as possible. These should be added at different heights and lengths too. Remember to add plenty underneath your design and at the sides to hide the floral foam. Add more foliage, if needed.
6. Finally, add long lengths of pampas grass on the sides and use smaller lengths throughout (you can break off pieces and tape them on to discarded stems - *see* page 32). Little pieces of pampas work beautifully to cover your floral foam but you can also cut off small pieces of eucalyptus (especially the stems with large leaves) to cover all your mechanics.

That completes our section on room decor designs. Now you have all the skills and ideas for table and room arrangements, ranging from super simple and chic bud vases all the way through to large floor-standing pieces. You can adjust the size and scale of these pieces to work for your space. Turn to page 137 for some ideas on how to style these arrangements in different ways for your event.

ITEMS USED IN THIS DESIGN

This is a gorgeous soft and muted pastel-toned colour story; a great example of how a few touches of soft colour can transform a neutral colour palette. I used soft pink, lilac and gold-dipped hydrangea to elevate this natural colour palette.

- **Base materials** – Floral foam and floral bind wire.
- **Preserved flowers and foliage** – Preserved eucalyptus cinerea and preserved gypsophila.
- **Large focal flowers** – Preserved hydrangea in two colours, and palm cups.
- **Dried stems** – A lovely variety including broom bloom, statice, lavender, bunny tails, pampas grass and wheat.

OPPOSITE: Adding a little draping fabric to a wooden arch can make the whole effect much more interesting. I use a cheesecloth-style fabric as it doesn't slip on the wooden arch and is much easier to get into the position you want, plus I love the texture of it.

Eucalyptus cinerea has varied size leaves which make it a really useful foliage stem to use. Cut off the lower part of the stem with the large leaves and save them for covering your foam when you have completed your arrangement.

This design can be mostly focused on the front and sides as the back will not be seen once it's hanging on the arch.

Using large focal blooms such as hydrangea and palm cups, I am quickly able to cover most of the floral foam. Keep some stems longer and stagger them so that the focal blooms spread out throughout your design and are not only clustered in the middle.

Pampas grass gets fluffier and paler the longer you leave it to dry out. Place the stems across radiators to get them to dry really quickly. After drying, give them a shake (a lot of fluff will come off!) and the final effect will be really bushy and fluffy.

I usually add a few more stems of pampas grass and any longer stems of foliage to my design once it is hanging in place. It's much easier to see how the design works, the shape of your arrangement and the positioning of key stems. Sometimes I also move one or two stems so they can be appreciated better once I see how it looks on its arch.

SHANNON BESTWICK, WEDDING AND EVENTS MANAGER

Shannon has worked in wedding and event management since 2018. She currently works at Haarlem Mill Wedding and Events, based in a seventeenth-century cotton mill in the Derbyshire Dales. Shannon has worked at Haarlem Mills for the last four years, managing their weddings and events, working with hundreds of couples to plan their special day.

Tell us a little about what a usual working day looks like for you?
No two days I work are ever the same. My days range from meetings with prospective couples, to wedding prep, to the wedding day itself and more. One moment, I'm in a heartfelt conversation with a couple, planning their dream day, and the next I'm scrubbing floors, rearranging decor or chasing after my lively six-year-old. There is a lot of preparation that goes on behind the scenes for a wedding, but the actual day itself is a long and busy day and I'm constantly on my feet, rushing from one task to another. Managing a wedding venue while balancing home life is a whirlwind but I wouldn't have it any other way.

What types of weddings and events do you work on?
At Haarlem Mill we cater for a wide variety of events ranging from weddings, funerals and wakes and corporate events to a range of different parties. Weddings involve the most preparation but can themselves range from simple events with just a small number of people to more elaborate days with hundreds of guests. Some couples want lots of guidance for putting their event together while others have strong ideas about what they want to create for themselves, so my work is really varied.

What floral design trends or room layout ideas are you seeing couples opt for?
Every wedding is completely different, each couple putting their own stamp on the venue, but there are a few trends that I see that I do think work really well for our venue space. All of these trends are pretty timeless ideas.

The first trend to mention is dried florals and pampas grass. Dried florals, especially pampas grasses, are hugely popular at Haarlem Mill. The neutral tone of the grasses and texture create a contrast to the hard lines of the venue, adding softness and a bohemian flair. I love it when couples really embrace the mood of the venue and choose florals that work well with the space. For this, installations suspended from the ceiling work really well or using an arch at the end of the aisle that can be moved later to other areas of the reception.

Secondly, I see a lot of foliage and greenery, which I love. Lush greenery, such as eucalyptus, creates a balance between the raw, urban elements of the space and natural beauty of the surrounding countryside. Greenery installations might line tables, hang from the ceiling or cover large statement pieces. We have permanent greenery installations on our wedding breakfast floor so it's always nice when couples consider this existing decoration and enhance it by mirroring this feature elsewhere in their wedding decor.

Finally, another favourite look is to keep things modern, minimalist and classic. A lot of my couples lean towards more contemporary, minimalist designs, maybe featuring asymmetric floral arrangements that tend to work really well with the venue's industrial vibe. These types of florals are a really nice contrast to the industrial and authentic features of the beautiful old and historic mill.

What kind of floral arrangements work best for your venue? Do you have any tips on how to integrate florals into your venue?
I think dried florals work particularly well here at Haarlem Mill as they are season-less and so work at any time of the year. Also, they are very low maintenance and on a wedding day they are easy to move around as they don't require water and are not affected by changes in temperature or weather (which is always a factor in Derbyshire). As a wedding coordinator who is incredibly busy during the wedding day, anything that makes my life easier is much appreciated. I also love it when the couple come back the next day and are able to take everything home with them; I hate seeing beautiful things go in the bin.

We have multiple floors within our space to decorate. Florals that can be moved about the venue and used in multiple places are always really useful. Ceremony backdrops that are either a hanging installation or use a frame or arch are particularly impactful. These look incredible at the end of the aisle and can then be used again downstairs behind your top table. The same goes for aisle decorations, such as chair ends or bud vases, which can be used along the banquet tables later for the reception.

Can you share a memorable wedding that has stood out to you and why?
One wedding that stands out to me was a beautiful autumnal wedding from last year. The bridesmaids all wore a burnt orange colour and the florals contained deep burgundy, orange and a soft pampas grass. The whole wedding felt really warm and cosy. The couple chose a wooden backdrop and the aisle was lined with lanterns and candles, creating a glowing ambience with lots of different natural textures. What made the wedding so special was how perfectly the couple embraced the season and how they incorporated pumpkins, a boozy hot chocolate station and sparklers to finish off the evening. The warm, inviting atmosphere created a memorable experience for everyone and it really stood out to me too.

Shannon Bestwick. (Photo: EKR Pictures)

Can you give us one piece of advice for people planning to DIY their own wedding or event?
My advice for a couple planning to DIY their wedding would be to plan early and start as soon as possible. DIY weddings do require a lot of time and you need to pay special attention to detail. Giving yourself time to plan and execute will reduce stress and help ensure that everything you are planning for runs smoothly and actually gets done. Don't try to take on too many tasks as you will just get overwhelmed. Definitely persuade family and friends to help you; not only will it lighten the load but it's always lovely to see family getting together before the wedding to prepare the space and put all their ideas into action. Finally, look at other weddings that have taken place at your venue and get ideas of what you think worked well and what you think you could have done better; this will help you use the space you have chosen to its full potential and avoid common pitfalls.

PART THREE: STYLE IT

Arrangements that are made to sit flat on the floor or on a table also work well sitting flat on top of plinths. You can make these in different sizes and scales to add further interest. Raising them up makes the most of each piece.

Finishing Touches

Now that you have created a concept, selected your florals, opted for a colour story and learnt how to make your chosen designs, next let's tackle how to present all of your knowledge in the most compelling way possible. In this last part of the book I will guide you through everything you need to think about in order to present your flowers in a rich and beautiful way. The finishing touches really are what will make your wedding or event stand out from the crowd.

As you are designing your floral arrangements, have a think about all the different ways they could be displayed and finished. You could really add some character to your designs with different vases and ribbons.

Vases are available in all sorts of shapes, styles and colours. Clear glass will show the stems of your arrangements so you will need to ensure they are cut neatly and that your design is created with the spiral technique, so it looks neat and tidy if it can be seen.

Vases and Other Vessels

Table arrangements could be displayed in a range of different vases – there are so many to choose from it's almost limitless. As a general rule, keep your vases smaller than you think. The smaller the vase opening is, the more compact your arrangement will be and the fewer flowers you will need to fill it. Larger vases require a lot of flowers if you don't want them to splay out and look too sparse. You might also need to pad the bottom of the vase with some paper if your stems aren't long enough, so consider this when choosing your vase – in this case, you would want to opt for something opaque so you can't see the paper at the bottom.

You could use a touch of coloured glass or look for vintage glass bottles, often available in abundance on Facebook Marketplace or other vintage shops. Bud vase arrangements look lovely in little vintage glass bottles, and using pre-loved items are a thoughtful eco-conscious choice. Choose colours for your vases that complement or add to your colour story. For example, boho luxe arrangements work well with white or clear glass and brightly coloured wildflower designs could look lovely in coloured glass vases.

The same concepts around colour and style apply to bowls and other wider opening vessels; these would just need to be filled with floral foam to secure your flowers. Bowls, vases or jars with straight edges could even be tied around the top edge with ribbon, hessian or string to add a little more detail. Just make sure that you have chosen your vessels before you start making your arrangements so that you can bear the shape in mind as you are creating and can cut the stems to the right length.

Ribbons and Strings

I absolutely love choosing my ribbons! This little finishing touch adds so much to a bouquet design. Satin ribbons have lovely clean edges that don't easily fray if you cut them with sharp scissors on a 45-degree angle. I love the sheen and the polish they add to my designs. If you opt for satin ribbons like me, ensure you choose a good-quality double-faced ribbon (shiny satin on both sides of the ribbon). Ribbon quality really does add a huge amount of value to your finished product so don't scrimp on this.

Lots of floral designers use silk habotai ribbons and, while they come in lovely naturally dyed colours, I find them a little too flimsy and they add too much cost. They also fray like crazy and catch easily on the dried stems. Consider other materials too – velvet ribbons add a nice additional texture and work especially well for autumn or winter weddings, or you can cut lengths of old shirts and use the fabric as ribbons.

As well as the type of ribbon you choose, you can go for a number of different colour options. Either match them to an item of clothing – ivory for bridal or various colours for bridesmaids' dresses – or match to the bouquet. Alternatively, you could opt for a contrast ribbon that makes a statement. It's also nice to use a couple of different colours mixed together for a slightly more eclectic look, especially if your bouquet is very colourful.

Ribbons come in many widths. My preference is 2.5cm-(1in-) wide ribbon as I find it works really well for both the bouquets and the matching buttonholes. You can mix and match widths for a more interesting look. I also cut the finished ribbons at different lengths to give the whole look extra dimension.

You might not like the polished and shiny look for your finishings. In this case, you could choose a more rustic look such as a hessian ribbon or string, which works well for barn weddings, outdoor events or venues with more rustic charm.

Pins and Bows

For buttonholes and pin-on corsages, I use a pin with a head so that they are easy to attach – pearl-headed pins are my go-to. There are many different pin options such as simple stud ends, diamanté or coloured pearl heads, but I like to go as simple as possible.

If I'm using a hessian ribbon, I also finish the bouquet with a pearl-headed pin. The hessian holds itself in place really well, and doesn't fray, so it will stay put nicely with just a pin and there is no need to glue it.

My satin ribbons are tied and left to trail on my bouquets, but you could think about using bows or pins as a finishing detail on your bouquets or corsages as another lovely added detail.

Many couples like to add a keepsake to their bouquets such as a little photo charm, a good luck horseshoe charm or even a 'something blue' charm. You can attach this with a few stitches of thread onto your ribbons.

Choosing the right colour ribbon can take your designs to the next level. Bright coloured ribbon on a rainbow bouquet adds a lovely touch, or think champagne ribbons on a beautiful natural boho bouquet. Mix and match colours for added opulence.

Finishing Your Bouquet

Once you have completed your bouquet design, finish it beautifully by tying it with ribbon or string. Over the years, I have trialled different methods for tying the ribbons or using pearl-headed pins to finish the look, but I have found that the simple knot looks the most effective and attractive. Recently, I have started tying my ribbons with bows, which adds another cute little detail.

I wrap all my bouquets with tissue paper and Kraft paper, finished with a ribbon and branded sticker. I never use cellophane or plastic of any kind as I want my wrappings to be recyclable. I also think brown Kraft paper looks lovely and works with all colour palettes. I change the colour of the tissue paper to match the flowers.

Adding Ribbon

I'm going to show you how to finish your bouquet with a satin ribbon. I prefer to use these as they are easier to work with, don't fray and have a beautiful sheen, which I think elevates your bouquet.

The Method

1. Once you have finalised your bouquet design and tied it with floral bind wire, you can cut your stems with some sharp secateurs. I usually cut the stems on a wedding bouquet about 14cm (5½in) down from the bind wire, but you can go shorter for bridesmaids' or flower girls' bouquets. Some bouquets, such as designs with long stems of pampas or really large bouquets, look more impactful with longer stems.
2. Once the stems are cut, tighten the bind wire again so that it securely holds the stems in place.
3. Add some floral tape to cover the bind wire and hold any smaller stems in place well. This also helps create a nice flat, clean surface for you to apply your ribbons on to.
4. Start at the front of your bouquet and fold the ribbon at a 45-degree angle. I like to keep a long length at the front of about 70cm (28in). This will be the finished length of all your ribbons, so you can make them longer or shorter, depending on the look you are after.
5. Wrap your ribbon around the bouquet two or three times until you have a sturdy and straight appearance, then take the two ends and tie a knot in them at the front of the bouquet. Use a second long length of ribbon and tie it around the bouquet (also in a knot) so you have four long lengths of ribbon.
6. Cut the ends of each of the lengths of ribbon at 45 degrees, to help avoid fraying. If you cut your ribbons at slightly different lengths, they will look more attractive as they hang down.

Be extra careful when cutting your bouquet stems. Don't cut too much off, as you can't go back. Try cutting the stems a little longer than you need at first, then holding your bouquet to see how it feels before you cut further.

Choose a bind wire colour that works best with your flowers. Green wire works well with foliage-heavy bouquets and sand brown wire works well for pale-coloured bouquets or those with a lot of different colours in them.

Floral tape helps shorter stems stay in place and cleans up the look of the bouquet. Sometimes little fluffy pampas ends extend all the way to the wire, so it is a good idea to smooth them down before you finish with ribbon.

Folding at a 45-degree angle ensures that the ribbon lies flat when you start to wrap it around the bouquet. You want to keep everything as flat and clean as possible for a refined finish.

Knotting your ribbons gives you a clean and simple look, but you could consider using a pin to secure your ribbon or adding a bow or charm. Bear in mind if you are using a lot of different lengths that each knot adds extra width to the finished look, which can start to get quite messy.

You will need very sharp scissors to cut your ribbons, otherwise they will catch and pull, fraying the edges.

Wrapping Your Bouquet

Here is a step-by-step guide on how to wrap bouquets in tissue and Kraft paper. It is a simple technique but you need to know a few little tricks, especially when it comes to folding the paper.

The Method

1. The trickiest part to get right is the folding of the paper. I use ready-cut sheets of Kraft paper for simplicity, but you can also cut lengths from a roll. The paper is approximately 35 × 50cm (14 × 20in) for a bridesmaid bouquet and 50 × 70cm (20 × 28in) for a wedding bouquet. Fold your paper in half on an angle, creating two 'points' on the top edge.
2. Repeat this folding technique for one or two pieces of tissue paper and lay it on top of the brown Kraft paper. Lay your bouquet in the middle with the break point of the stems (or where you have tied your bouquet) sitting just below the paper.
3. Fold the papers around your bouquet and bunch the paper at the bottom. This will look a little rough but it will be covered with ribbons later. Squash the paper against the stems with your hand.

HOLDING YOUR BOUQUET

This might sound like a crazy thing to spend time discussing but after all the hard work of creating your bouquet, it really does make a difference how you hold it to show it in the most optimal way.

Hold your bouquet too high and you are covering your beautiful clothes; hold it too low and it looks somewhat strange. So, my advice is for you to hold your bouquet with slightly bended arms and at the bottom of your torso. Then tilt your bouquet slightly forward to show off the blooms in the most beautiful way. You don't need to show the stems to your guests; they want to see the flowers in all their glory. Let the ribbons hang down beautifully.

4. Lay the bouquet down and cut a 70cm (28in) length of ribbon. Tie it around the bunched and flattened paper to secure it in place.
5. Use a stapler to secure the papers at the top edge.
6. Add a sticker to cover the staple, and your bouquet will be wrapped and looking beautiful!

Craft paper is affordable and looks good with all colour palettes. You can wrap your bouquets just in tissue or with special papers if you prefer, or even write messages to your bridal party on the paper.

Adding multiple layers of paper makes the finished look a little more special. You could use a number of different colours together for a more interesting finish. Think about matching back to the flowers or to your bridesmaids' dresses.

The heavier the weight of paper you use, the harder it is to bunch up nicely. Don't use stiff papers as they will squash your flowers and make them appear flat at the back of the bouquet.

Prepare all the items in advance so you are not trying to cut lengths of ribbon while holding your wrapped bouquet. You can use floral bind wire here if you are looking for a simpler look.

It is not essential to staple your papers. You can just leave them to open on their own; the ribbon you have tied it with will hold it in place.

I use branded stickers for finishing the wrapping, but you could use any kind of sticker. A little heart sticker or one that is printed with your name would look really special.

TARA KNOTT, WEDDING STYLIST AND EVENTS DESIGNER

Tara has been curating beautiful spaces, weddings, events and more since 2012. Her work has been featured in *HELLO!* magazine, *Save the Date* magazine, Green Wedding Shoes and Love my Dress.

Tell us a little about yourself.
I am a wedding stylist and event designer based in Derby, specialising in curating modern and stylish weddings and events across the East Midlands. We offer a range of services, including full wedding styling, venue dressing, prop hire and planning for commercial shoots. My background has always been in events, deciding to take the leap into setting up my own business when I was on maternity leave thirteen years ago. Having studied theatre arts and later event management, I had a keen interest in how people behave in different spaces. I am fortunate enough to get to create some stunning installations and set-ups and work with incredible suppliers.

Do your designs work with your couples' personalities?
When it comes to event planning and styling, working with a couple's personalities is key to creating a design that truly feels like their day. I always start with a thorough consultation with the couple to understand who they are, their interests, and what makes them unique as a couple. This means asking questions about their likes, dislikes and the atmosphere they want for their event. Whether they want something fun and quirky or elegant and classic, understanding their personalities helps me work out every detail. After that, I start selecting colours, textures and design elements that would work. For example, if a couple loves the outdoors, I might incorporate elements like greenery and rustic florals. If they're more of a minimal style, I might lean towards modern decor and clean lines.

What are the key elements in a styling plan?
Using colours that complement the theme sets the tone for the event, so I always get couples to consider if they are choosing a colour because it is on trend or because it reflects their personality. Next I consider the venue layout and how it can be styled to consider the flow of people. I wouldn't want to set up an elaborate backdrop that interferes with how the day runs and gets in the way. I choose florals, centrepieces and decor items to match the theme and complement the colour palette.

Designing the table settings is one of my favourite parts of the job. I always consider the kind of food being served as this impacts the space on the tables – if you are opting for sharing food then we need to make sure there is space for everything.

Backdrops and draping for the ceremony that can be repurposed throughout the space to be enjoyed all day. Designing stationery and signage that not only guides guests but also ties into the style and theme. Deciding on the elements that will be repurposed around the space to make the most out of all decor items. When all these elements come together thoughtfully, they create a well-coordinated, engaging experience for guests that makes sense.

How do you balance trends with timeless styles?
I often have couples wanting to have a trend-led wedding but deep down their style is more timeless. The best looks feel authentic, so I always recommend you use trends that resonate with you, but don't force them if they don't align with your natural style. On-trend elements like disco balls don't need to be everywhere; if you want a more timeless ceremony, save them for the party floor. That way you will look back on photos and still be happy with your choices.

What role do flowers play in your event styling?
Flowers play a huge role in event styling, acting as both a visual focal point and a way to enhance the

Tara Knott. (Photo: Amy Elizabeth Photography.)

overall mood or theme of an event. Flowers have a unique ability to evoke emotion. Soft, romantic blooms like roses or peonies can create a delicate, intimate atmosphere, while vibrant, bold florals like sunflowers or tropical arrangements can bring an energetic, lively vibe. Flowers are a great way to reinforce the event's colour scheme. Large floral installations at entrances, or as part of a stunning backdrop, elevate everything.

What are your tips for choosing floral arrangements that work with different venues?
Here are some tips I have picked up along the way. In a spacious venue you can go big with your florals. Think large installations or floral arches. These elements will stand out in a big room and ensure that your floral designs don't get lost.

For smaller spaces, opt for more understated arrangements such as low centrepieces or smaller groups of flowers to avoid overwhelming the space.

If you're hosting an event in a venue with traditional decor, like a grand hotel or a church, classic floral arrangements, such as roses, will work beautifully. For a sleek, modern venue with minimalistic or industrial details (think lofts or warehouses), you can lean into more contemporary florals such as bold, sculptural arrangements. In more rustic settings, such as barns or gardens, wildflower-style arrangements are a perfect choice. Think about the colours of the venue – its walls, flooring and furniture. Choose florals that either contrast or complement what is already there.

Can you share a previous example of a floral design that transformed a wedding or event you worked on?
One piece of work I am proud of is the styling imagery for this book – a collaboration between Sarah and myself. We created a large, draped installation with festoon lighting and an abundance of floral arrangements that we could then reuse around the venue. This backdrop worked so well in the space because of the high ceilings, and the plinths with florals elevated the overall look. The combination of textured fabrics, lights and florals created a wow factor for the space.

How do you use colour to enhance a space?
Colour is an incredibly powerful tool in event styling because it can completely transform the mood and feel of a space. By using bold or contrasting colours, you can draw attention to specific features or areas in the space. For example, if you're working with a neutral backdrop, using vibrant pops of colour in key places (like a bright red centrepiece or deep blue cushions) can make those elements become the focal point of the room. Using variations of one colour can create a cohesive, harmonious look. For example, different shades of green can add depth while maintaining a calming atmosphere. Playing into the seasons and using seasonal floral colours is a great way to make a venue feel either cosy, or light and springy.

What advice would you give an aspiring florist on how to present their florals in the best way possible?
Presenting florals in the best possible way goes beyond just creating beautiful arrangements – it is about showing your work in a way that highlights your style. Always keep in mind where the florals will be displayed – whether it's in a ceremony or on a table. The type of flowers, arrangement size and colour palette should complement the event's mood, location and style. Think about the places where the florals will be placed. You want your florals to complement the space rather than compete with it.

Use social media to tell the story behind your work; couples love to see where your ideas come from.

What common mistakes do you see when someone is styling their own event?
I often see people choosing a design that doesn't align with the venue's aesthetic. Placing modern, minimalistic decor in a historic or ornate venue just seems off. Also using too many clashing or mismatched colours can make the event feel disjointed and chaotic. Often, people choose colours based on what they like without thinking about how they'll flow together. People commonly tend to overdo things. Less is often more – focus on key areas where decor will have the most impact, like the entrance, centrepieces or focal walls. Forgetting about the practical elements of the event, such as seating, is another common mistake. For example, placing large floral arrangements in the middle of tables can make it really difficult for the guests to see each other.

Probably the most common mistake is to leave too much of the styling to the last minute. Start planning early and give yourself plenty of time to gather materials, create your arrangements and set up. Allow time for trial runs, especially for complex arrangements like floral installations or large-scale centrepieces.

If you're styling your own event, remember to keep things simple and pay attention to all the little details.

Three floral arrangements are all that is needed here to create a stunning backdrop when paired with fabric drapery, plinths, strings of lights, candles and disco balls. These arrangements can then be moved and reused in other areas of your event.

Dressing the Room

There are a number of ways you can make your flowers more useful and reduce the number of items you need to make by reusing your flowers for multiple parts of your day. In order to decide what you need for your venue, think about the order of events and imagine yourself as you move through your day. Consider which items will need to remain in their place and which can be moved and used more than once.

It's always nice to have something at your entrance to show your guests a little snapshot of what your event is going to look like. Depending on your budget and the time you have allocated to create your flowers, you can have a large floor-standing arrangement, a table centrepiece or little bud vases. You could use all three together or you could use one or more items to create your installation, depending on the size of the space you would like to fill.

Next, imagine you are making your way into the venue. Are you planning a wedding? If so, here is the time where you would head down the aisle. Do you want the whole aisle adorned with flowers, with additional flowers at the end of the aisle? Do you want a wow, maximum impact floral installation such as an arch or a flower cloud? Do you have a registrar's table that you would like to dress? All of the items used in your wedding aisle can be repurposed for the rest of the day, so try to imagine what they could be used for later.

Perhaps you are creating florals for a dinner or birthday party. If so, would you like flowers on your food tables? You could go for an impactful look with table centrepieces throughout or a simpler look with little vases of flowers. Finally, do you have other spaces you want to decorate such as cake tables, memory tables, gift tables, photobooths or disco signage? All of these areas could be dressed with little vases, table centrepieces or meadow floor-standing arrangements.

The beginning of the aisle is an area that often gets forgotten about, but by putting a few arrangements here you can really transform the space. Think about your first photo as a married couple and how the flowers will frame that image beautifully.

Placing Bud Vases

The small but mighty bud vase! This little gem is not only easy and affordable to make but it can be used in so many different ways to elevate your event or look beautiful in your home. You have chosen your vases to match your flowers or your event space; now let's consider a few different ways that you can use these arrangements.

Being so small and light, bud vases can easily be moved about the venue, so let's first use them for your ceremony space – they add a lovely finishing touch to your registrar's table or altar equivalent. Pop a couple of vases (use varying heights for more interest) on the end of the table, along with a registrar's long arrangement, and your end of aisle will look stunning. Also use a couple of bud vases at the foot of any sign that you might have adorning your space – perhaps you have an 'unplugged ceremony' sign or a sign to advise guests of where they are to sit – pop a couple of buds on the floor next to this and you'll really amp up your signage.

You can also place bud vases at the end of the aisle in little groups along with candles, or all the way down the aisle for maximum impact. I have used bud vases in pretty much any place we can squeeze them: table plans, welcome areas, card tables, cake tables... the list goes on.

After you have used your bud vases for the ceremony, you can reuse them for your wedding breakfast tables. They are perfect in groups of two or three on round tables, or placed periodically down long banquet tables. Don't forget to use a couple at each end of your sweetheart or top table too; along with candles, they add a little something to make that table area really special.

Finally, take a look about your space and see if there are any areas that you feel need a little added something – perhaps beside some shelves or disco balls. Pop bud vases anywhere you think could use a hand until you've used everything you have created.

Bud vases look lovely in groups of three, but if you are also using candles you can reduce them to two plus a candle to create a lovely little set-up. Use two different designs for your bud vases so the look is more eclectic.

Adding some fabric that tones with your bud vases makes the centre of your table look so much more special. Pillar candles create ambience and protect the naked flames from touching the flowers.

Finding little nooks to place bud vases in adds a touch of whimsy to your event, especially if your venue has lots of old character and charm that would benefit from a touch of colour.

Disco balls are having a moment right now but there are lots of different varieties to choose from. Opt for colours and sizes that work with the tones of your florals, and your event will really stand out.

Sweetheart tables are a gorgeous way of creating a little space to share some one-on-one time with your partner. You can concentrate a lot of flowers together to make this space really special. Think floor arrangements as well as table arrangements, candles, fabric and bud vases.

Using Table Centrepieces

Table centrepieces are absolutely perfect for their intended use – tables – because they look wonderful from all angles. They are a sumptuous design for the middle of a table, and styled with candles, table number signs, favours and name cards, your tables will come to life. In addition, there are other fantastic uses for these arrangements. They look lovely moved to the side of the room after your sit-down meal, or used by the side of your bar area or cake table. They also work well on top of a stand or crate at your welcome area, next to your welcome sign.

Meadow Arrangement

The meadow arrangement is a tall, long and dramatic piece that has multiple uses and gives you a little drama. I like to use meadow arrangements at the beginning of the aisle and then reuse them after the ceremony. They work wonderfully placed on the floor, such as adorning a disco-party banner on a dance floor, or placed on top of a wooden letter display inside the venue.

This large-scale arrangement can be amazing if used in a welcome area. Sometimes smaller arrangements can get a little lost in this part of your event, so it can be a good idea to really go for this and make something quite large to entice your guests as they enter the space.

Registrar's Arrangement

This beautiful floral piece is a really useful item that can make more than one area look special. Its most common use is adorning the registrar's table at the end of the aisle, then moved to decorate the centre of the top table or sweetheart table. Its size and shape make it perfect for not obstructing the view of the couple during speeches. You can up the appeal of this arrangement by using a few additional bud vases or adding some colourful fabric draping underneath it. Using candles near it is also possible as it is such a low arrangement that it doesn't come anywhere near the open flames.

Banners featuring wording can make your space more personal while adding much-needed textures and colours. Perhaps you have a favourite song you want to mention on a banner or a phrase that is special to you. These items take your wedding up a notch.

Dried and preserved flowers need to be kept out of sunlight for their colour to remain vivid, but you can place them next to windows to show off their beautiful colour if it is only for a short time.

Positioning Floor-Standing Arrangements

Perhaps the most versatile of all the larger pieces, floor-standing arrangements can be used on their own, in groups or pushed together to make larger arrangements. With as little as three of these arrangements, you can make an incredible look to use throughout your space. Start by using three arrangements at the end of your aisle, either placed on the floor or on something to give them height such as a wooden plinth or stand. Placing them at varying heights adds more interest, but you can also make these arrangements in different scales to add further dimensions to your final look.

Pop one of these large pieces at a welcome area, perhaps sitting on a stand or crate, to entice your guests with the beautiful flowers they can expect when they enter your venue. Floor-standing arrangements also look lovely at the beginning of your aisles, on the floor next to the first row of chairs. This will give you a beautiful look as you exit your aisle once you are married – perfect for the photos.

After your ceremony, you can use two of these arrangements pushed together to create an even larger piece that can sit at the foot of your sweetheart or top table. This works especially well if you make these pieces quite tall. Just bear in mind where and when you will be using each piece so that you make the size work for multiple locations in your venue.

Use varying heights of plinths, paint them different colours and use different-sized arrangements on them to add variety and interest to your displays. Allow a little space between your stands so the flowers have room to show themselves off.

If your arrangements are planned to sit up on a stand, crate or plinth, think about the bottom so that it looks beautiful, even if it is at eye level. Make sure you cover the floral foam but also consider having a few stems drape down and cascade away from the rest of the flowers.

Floor-standing arrangements can be pushed together to make one much larger piece with lots of visual impact. You can create a whole meadow of flowers in this way by using three or four floor pieces separately and then again together.

Taking It to the Next Level

Let's style up your event with more than just the flowers. You've created table arrangements and floor-standing pieces to be used in lots of different places during your event, but you can make these items look even more special with a few simple added touches.

Welcome Signs and Areas

In addition to your floral arrangements, add a little fabric drapery, a couple of candles and a lovely sign and you have created a perfect little welcome to your event. You can place your flowers at different heights – use boxes or crates to achieve this. It's always nice to have different-sized arrangements placed together, so perhaps you have a table centrepiece on one side and two little bud vases on the other side, with different designs in each.

For flowers to extend tall and slightly cover signage, you will need to use long, sturdy, strong stems such as foliage, achillea or pampas grass.

Wedding Aisle

Here you can make a few items look beautiful or go all out and really wow your guests. Bear in mind that this area is often cleared and repurposed as a dance floor, so you might want your arrangements to stay in place for later in the day, or move them to other areas.

Your aisle can be brought to life with candles or lanterns. Even if you aren't allowed naked flames for your event, you can buy very good LED lights that will still give off a lovely warm look and create ambience. Placing candles at the foot of your aisle, with little bud vases among them, adding fabric draping and positioning floor-standing arrangements on stands or plinths, will create a heavenly backdrop. You could use vintage tables or plant stands, or make wooden plinths and paint them in beautiful colours. Perhaps you have a flower cloud hanging at the end of your aisle and want to keep the rest of the styling minimal – just a few lanterns on the last row of chairs gives a little more interest.

Registrar's or altar tables at the end of the aisle look lovely with some fabric draped over them and a floral arrangement in the middle. Add even more interest with some lovely matching candles and a couple more bud vases. Just make sure that the fabric is long enough to 'pool' slightly as it hits the floor – this looks opulent and intentional.

Floor-standing arrangements work beautifully down the aisle as they give the impression that the flowers are growing out of the ground naturally. You could use these arrangements all the way down the aisle for maximum impact or place them at every other row.

Welcome areas look lovely even with one small floral arrangement if you style them up with lots of little items such as candles, lanterns, signage and fabric drapery.

Tables

Think first about the table shape you are decorating. Long banquet-style tables look lovely with lengths of fabric all the way down the centre. Place your floral arrangements every now and then along with candles, name cards, place settings, table numbers and favours, if you are having them. The tables soon fill up, but including more textures and tones adds interest.

Round tables look lovely with a centrepiece on top of some matching fabric, or bud vases in groups of three or five – odd numbers always look better. Remember that people need to see over your decor to talk to one another so either don't make the arrangements too tall or make them narrow or wispy so people can see around and through them.

Large Installations

Just because your floral arrangement itself has a huge impact – perhaps it is a large piece that is a focal part of your day – that doesn't mean that you don't have an opportunity to add something extra to it. I have loved creating huge hanging flower bomb designs and adding hanging disco balls to them. Or a large arrangement on an arch at the end of an aisle, or behind a table, looks so much more amazing with some carefully draped fabric or hanging tealights. Think also about placing more arrangements on the floor next to an arch, with candles among it.

YOUR EVENT IS OVER... NOW WHAT?

No matter which kind of designs you choose, you can keep them! So, have a think about what you would like to use them for after your event; you can give them away as gifts, use them for your home or save them for a future event.

Flower clouds can be repurposed to hang above a dining table or as a headboard in a master bedroom. Table arrangements can be used for sideboards, side tables or dining tables, and long registrar's arrangements can be placed in unused fire grates or used as Christmas table centrepieces.

One of my couples put little thank you stickers onto each bud vase and every guest got one to take home. Another put buttonholes into a deep frame and hung it in their living room, while another used a flower crown as a wreath for her baby daughter's bedroom. The ideas are endless!

Round tables fill up very fast once you add all the other little finishing touches. Gather everything you plan to use before you start so you can make sure the table won't get too crowded, and remember to plan for tableware and glasses.

Using flowers in unexpected places can add whimsy and fun to your event and surprise your guests. Making your flowers in little wooden trays means that they are easy to move about and to balance on different surfaces.

Final Words

I've taken you on a journey on these pages that has taken me years to master. I hope you have been able to absorb all you need to get creative and start your projects with confidence and ease. I can't stress enough how important preparation is; spend time researching, coming up with a concept and colour palette, and thinking about your event space and how you can best fill it. The more research you do, the easier the creation will be. Make mood boards and reference them throughout the process. It's easy to get sidetracked when you are creating; a quick look back at your concept and you'll keep yourself on track.

Be Bold and Go for Those Colours

Don't be afraid of colour. It can really bring your event to life; it can complement the space or the people; it can tell its own story. Colour makes people happy – no one will feel sad if they see a stunning, bright and colourful colour palette, and you will have so much fun putting together a beautiful colour story. Remember, if a colour doesn't look quite right, you can always remove it until you are happy with your palette, but play around with different combinations.

More is Most Definitely More

My most important advice would be: *more is more*! You can never create too many arrangements or have too many flowers or decor items. More colour, more flowers, more pieces... you won't regret having more than you need.

Develop Your Own Style

Allow some time to practise and develop your own style. You will soon discover what you like and what you don't, and your ideas will become more concrete. This will give you the confidence to complete your project with ease. If something feels like your vibe, it is! So, go with the flow and learn a little about yourself along the way.

Make Mistakes

It's OK to make mistakes; that's part of the creative process. Just make sure you allow yourself enough time – if you have time to repair any issues, all will be well. The best thing about dried flowers is that nothing will go bad if you don't use it in a timely manner; you have time to make the changes you need. Rushing will cause things to get missed or items to not be finished properly. Consider how best to spend your time, rope in family and friends, but most of all, have fun!

When I did my own wedding flowers I loved it so much that I didn't notice any of the imperfections I see when I look now at the pictures. All I thought about was how proud I was of myself and how much money I had saved! So, grab your tools and your ideas and go for it. You can do it too!

Brightly coloured flowers could be matched back to their surroundings. Use your event space as your starting point for your colour and concept to ensure a cohesive look.

Further Information

Useful Websites

Sarah Ogden
www.horseshoeflowers.com

Mirlah Richardson
www.mirland.co

Shannon Bestwick
https://haarlemmill.co.uk

Tara Knott
www.taraknott.co.uk

Stockists

If you are lucky enough to live near a flower market, you should see what is available for immediate pickup. Some have whole sections of dried flowers – see their colours and look at different combinations next to each other. I order my flowers from the following two Dutch online companies. You can create an account easily, browse photos and order directly for delivery. They have a minimum spend for free delivery and a live catalogue of what is available:

Hoek Flowers
hoekflowers.com

Van VLIET Flower Group
jvanvliet.com

UK Suppliers

Atlas Flowers
atlasflowers.co.uk
An amazing selection of dried and preserved flowers and preserved foliage, as well as floral sundries including papers, foam and some tools.

Barn Florist
barnflorist.co.uk
Specialising in preserved flowers, although they also carry dried varieties. They have an amazing selection of preserved hydrangeas and roses.

Fora Nature
foranature.com
Fantastic supplier for preserved flowers. They carry specialist varieties such as dahlia, orchids and carnations.

Hobbycraft
hobbycraft.co.uk
Great for tools, papers, vases and a wide range of ribbons in lovely colours.

Homebase
homebase.co.uk
For chicken wire and other useful tools.

Trevor Green Floral Sundries
floralsundries.com
Great for reasonably priced glassware, wires and papers as well as a small selection of grasses and dried flowers.

US Suppliers

A Floral
afloral.com
A gorgeous selection of dried and preserved florals in a beautiful palette of colours.

Home Depot
homedepot.com
Perfect for chicken wire, stub wires and tools.

Idle Wild Floral
idlewildfloral.com
A lovely selection of dried and preserved flowers arranged by colour story.

Michaels
michaels.com
A treasure trove for creative items such as foam, papers and ribbons at good prices.

Roxanne's Dried Flowers
roxannesdriedflowers.com
A wide selection of dried flowers and grasses as well as preserved flowers such as roses and hydrangea.

Index

First published in 2025 by
The Crowood Press Ltd
Ramsbury, Marlborough
Wiltshire SN8 2HR

enquiries@crowood.com
www.crowood.com

© Sarah Ogden 2025

All rights reserved. No part of this publication may be reproduced or transmitted in any form or by any means, electronic or mechanical, including photocopy, recording, or any information storage and retrieval system, without permission in writing from the publishers.

British Library Cataloguing-in-Publication Data
A catalogue record for this book is available from the British Library.

For product safety-related questions, contact:
productsafety@crowood.com

ISBN 978 0 7198 4561 1

The right of Sarah Ogden to be identified as author of this work has been asserted by her in accordance with the Copyright, Designs and Patents Act 1988.

Typeset by Envisage IT
Cover design by Sergey Tsvetkov
Printed and bound in India by Thomson Press India Ltd

Dedication
For Ada and Sammy

Acknowledgements
Thank you to my husband Ben, who supported me financially and emotionally as I took a leap of faith and left a good-paying job to retrain in floristry. I can't thank you enough for never complaining about the dried flower dust all over our house, boxes in every inch of spare space, trips to the post office or mad dashes to my studio when I have forgotten something. Thank you for listening to every idea I have ever had and for saying 'why not?'

To my family who have always supported everything I've ever done and told me I could do whatever I wanted, thank you. Especially to my sister, Rachael, who also doubles up as my best friend, business coach and mentor. Thank you for the hours spent listening to my ideas and for giving me the confidence to go for things as well as putting me on the right path numerous times. No matter what I do, the next question will always be 'what's next?' and I'm very grateful for it.

To all my couples who have trusted me with their wedding flowers, I have loved every single wedding I have created for you and I can't wait to create more floral dreams.

To the many suppliers who I have worked with along the way, whether it's photographers who have kindly shared their beautiful images with me, wedding stylists who have taken my flowers and styled them to the next level, content creators, event managers, venue co-ordinators and many more, thank you.

A special thank you to Holly Booth who shot my branding photography, helping me set the tone for my business, and who also shot a lot of the beautiful photography for this book.

Thank you to Mirlah Richardson and Tara Knott who helped me style up and photograph the beautiful wedding venue, The West Mill, with all my florals so I could show you how to style it all. Also, thank you to Becky Payne Photography who allowed me to use her lovely images of our epic flower cloud installation.

Finally, thank you to Crowood for taking a chance on this book, supporting me through the process, calmly answering my many emails for ideas on layouts for the book, title changes and those 'middle of the night' brainwaves. Thank you for making this dream become a reality.